CASH OR CREDIT?

A Nuts and Bolts Guide to Effective Credit Management

Paul D. Zuelke

PennWell Publishing Company
1421 South Sheridan/P.O. Box 1260
Tulsa, Oklahoma 74101

Library of Congress Cataloging-in-Publication Data

Zuelke, Paul D.
Cash or credit?: a nuts and bolts guide to effective credit management/Paul D. Zuelke.
p. cm—(Dental economics)
Includes index.
ISBN 0-87814-338-6: $39.95
1. Dentistry—Practice. 2. Credit—Management. 3. Dental economics. I. Title. II. Title. Series: Dental economics (Tulsa, Okla.)
RK58.Z84 1989 89-2913
617.6′0068′1—dc19 CIP

Printed in the United States of America

1992

ACKNOWLEDGMENTS

Dr. Elizabeth Neeld. You supported me, you acknowledged me, and most importantly you held me accountable to keep my word.

Linnea. You corrected my errors, perfected my manuscript, and made sense out of nonsense.

Lenora. You created the space that made this book possible.

To you all, I give my most sincere and heartfelt thanks.

CONTENTS

Section II: Nuts and Bolts

INTRODUCTION

I originally became a consultant because I firmly believed improper use of credit management and ineffective accounts receivable control were seriously damaging the well-being and quality of life of the health care community. I felt if I could effectively teach what I knew about credit management, something positive would happen.

Many years later and with hundreds of clients throughout the United States and Canada, I have come to two major conclusions. First, my initial assumption that effective credit management would enhance the well-being of the health care community was accurate; and second, I have not even scratched the surface in delivering my message to the dental community, much less the medical, chiropractic, or other health care communities.

My purpose in writing this book is two-fold: 1) to provide a context — a background — in the philosophy and value of effective credit management in the dental office, and 2) to provide specific "nuts and bolts" recommendations that will, when implemented, serve as a guide for the credit policies of the practices and persons reading this book.

The goal of this book is to assist dentists and their staff members in the development of an efficient credit management program through the implementation of the recommendations listed herein. As a result, the practice will experience consistently high cash flow, low delinquency, low accounts receivable, excellent case acceptance, and a satisfying growth. The greatest benefit will be the impeccable quality of life within the practice.

SECTION I:

PHILOSOPHY

INTRODUCTION

If you were to follow the progress of the dental office from the early 1800's, through the 1900's and up to today, you would see tremendous differences in how dentistry was practiced.

Many years ago, the town dentist was also the town barber. The early dentist had absolutely no dental education other than the education provided by experience, and the thought of reconstructive or restorative dentistry was far in the future. Dentists of old provided strictly pain relief, primarily through extractions!

With territories becoming states and with territorial governments becoming organized state governments, regulation of the business and the practice of dentistry became commonplace. Educational requirements were established and strengthened over the years. Today's doctors graduating from dental school have the finest qualifications in history.

The clinical tools of the trade of the 1800s and early 1900s are no longer used today and, in fact, can very often be seen in glass cases as curiosities or collectors' items in many dental offices. Full-mouth reconstructions using the most modern materials including porcelain, polymers, and implant surgeries are commonplace today, yet they were unheard of and inconceivable only fifty years ago.

The dentist from 1900, transported in a time machine to a dental office of today, would probably not believe that he could be in a dental office. At least, that would be the case if he were transported into a clinical setting. However, if the doctor of 1900 were transported to the administrative setting of today's dental office, he would find himself right at home. The modern American doctor takes great pains and incurs great expense to use only the most modern and efficient clinical procedures and to utilize the most well-trained clinical staff. Yet he often handles credit management and accounts receivable control in his office in the same manner used fifty or even a hundred years ago.

Also, many doctors have found to their dismay that the techniques, policies, and procedures used in their office to handle credit and collections when the practice was small are no longer effective. Numerous outside factors now have impact on the health of a dental practice — factors that fifty years ago either did not exist or were not an issue to be considered by a dentist. A partial list of these factors would include competition from other dentists, commercial storefront dentistry, capitation plans, PPOs, closed-panel insurance, state and federal regulations governing credit and collection, the economy, consumerism and consumer protection, malpractice, patients' dental I.Q., and bankruptcy rates that are 25 times higher than they were.

Basically, the administrative needs of the modern dental practice have increased right along with the clinical, yet the administrative side of a dental practice has been a weak sister to the clinical side. Often thousands of dollars will be spent on a new clinical product, but a needed copy machine or a seminar oriented to the administrative side of the practice will have a low priority.

The material in this book is designed to bring the administrative end of your practice into the late 20th century and prepare for your aggressive entrance into the 21st century.

There is a tremendous misconception common among dentists and that is: *the way things have always been in dentistry is the way things are going to continue to be.* This misconception is common only when the topic is the administrative end of the practice. However, there are no such thoughts when discussing the clinical side of the practice; not when the doctor readily spends thousands of dollars on a new panographic x-ray machine, a new fiber-optic system, or a new ultra-modern dental chair.

Unfortunately, even the most enlightened dental schools are providing a minimum of education regarding the administrative operation of a dental practice. That education seems to be exclusively in the area of accounting and setting up bookkeeping systems. Today's dentists are well-prepared to enter the practice of dentistry, but ill-prepared to enter the "business" of dentistry. Since they have little technology or training, they quickly resign themselves to the aforementioned misconception — the way things have always been is the way they will continue to be.

These misconceptions are caused by "brain damage." Fortunately it is brain damage that, over a short period of time, can be repaired with wonderful and powerful results for the dental practice.

At this point, you may just want to think of it as a "what if." For instance, what if it were possible to grant credit efficiently, to have almost 100% case acceptance and to always have a 100% collection rate? What if it were possible to have little or no delinquency in the office? What if your staff could sell dentistry more efficiently and more successfully than you could yourself? What if your no-show/cancellation rate were less than 2% of scheduled appointments?

I suspect the answer to these "what if" questions would be that you would have the highest possible quality of life within a practice that enjoyed high productivity, high net income and, more important, a high level of job satisfaction.

CHAPTER 1

PATIENT MANAGEMENT MYTHS: ERRONEOUS THOUGHTS WHICH PREEMPT A SUCCESSFUL COLLECTIONS PROCESS

The erroneous thinking presented through these myths is an example of why the doctors and staff members of many dental offices in this country are not experiencing more inner satisfaction, joy, and financial success in their work. These errors in thinking actually preempt the doctor from having an opportunity to enhance the quality of life in his practice — for himself or his staff. This wrong thinking significantly affects how the doctor approaches and thinks about the collection process and his practice as a whole. Let's look at a few of these myths, and I think you will recognize what I mean.

MYTH #1

No-shows, last-minute cancellations, tardy patients, patients who do not accept our diagnosis, patients who fail to make their payments or who make partial or token payments, are all patient-related problems that are inherent in the practice of dentistry. And, we must learn to live with them.

Comments:

I call this thinking "brain damage," because there is absolutely no basis for this misconception in the real world. The evidence is all around us of practices completely free of the types of problems referred to in this misconception; therefore, the problems *cannot* be inherent in the business. A decision to continue to live with these problems does not come from believing the problems are unsolvable, but rather from believing the steps to solve the problems create a situation that would be uncomfortable for the doctor. The decision to remain comfortable takes precedence over the decision to solve problems.

A real belief in this myth paralyzes the practice. This belief system will prevent you from exploring potential solutions to the problem and, of course, this belief will prevent you from reaching the state of the art in dentistry that is possible.

An Example:

I had a client in Portland who, in late 1981, was producing approximately $30,000 per month. His overhead was approximately 60%. His production per hour worked was just over $200, and he was working 32 hours a week. His receivables were $90,000 (three months production), and his aged receivables (most of which were delinquent) were approximately $50,000. His no-show/cancellation rate was approaching 25% of scheduled patients.

This doctor was unhappy and frustrated with the state of his practice. Yet, rather than having "brain damage" and believing that the way things were is the way things had to be, he was willing to take whatever steps were necessary to repair the problem. He implemented numerous changes with respect to policy and procedure in his office, even though many of them were uncomfortable. Sometimes it meant a patient was unable to receive the care he had diagnosed, or that a patient who was delinquent was asked to leave the practice.

Today this doctor enjoys a practice that is producing at the rate of close to $500 per hour. His no-show/cancellation rate is less than 3% of scheduled patients. His accounts receivable are $80,000 (one and one-half months production), and his aged receivables have fallen to 25% of his total receivables. For this doctor, there were no problems that were "inherent" in the business.

MYTH #2

I am at the mercy of my competition or the local economy. My fees need to be low so that my patients can afford me.

Comments:

If this were so, after many years of traveling throughout the country and visiting thousands of dentists, I would have seen at least a few examples of successful, profitable low-fee practices. However, the opposite is true. Practices that are achieving at the highest possible level — not only in gross production and net income, but also in new patient flow, overall patient satisfaction, and staff morale — are practices that have fees in the top 5–10% of doctors in their community. Topnotch practices are not low-fee practices but are practices that have developed large numbers of patients with confidence in the doctor, and who feel loved by the doctor and staff. These qualities are much more valuable than low fees and price incentives.

If you are committed to quality of practice and quality of life within the practice, the last type of patient you want to attract is the type who would be attracted because of low prices. Most patients you consider "shoppers" are not shopping for price nearly as much as for an experience. Since there is no technical difference between the quality of a crown done by a doctor charging $700 per unit and the quality of a crown done by a doctor charging $300 per unit, the unique thing you have to offer is the quality of *personal care* you provide and the overall experience of your practice that you create.

An Example:

I have two clients who practice less than 100 feet from each other in a small town in my home state of Oregon. The town has primarily a lumber economy and was hit very hard in the recession of the late 70s and early 80s. Unemployment was high throughout the state, but it was especially high in this town.

One of these clients had relatively low fees and suffered a downturn in productivity during this recession. The other practice, which was literally across the street, had gross productivity that increased by over 20% during the same period, and yet this second practice had fees that were substantially higher than the first.

This situation occurs regularly in communities throughout the country. Patients are interested in a quality product for a reasonable price, and they are interested in the quality of the experience they will have in a practice. If you have done your job of nurturing your patients, supporting them and being certain they sense your care and concern, they will stay with your practice. They will accept your diagnosis and will refer their friends to your practice with little regard for the amount of your fees.

MYTH #3

I have an obligation to provide care to any patient who requests it.

Comments:

This misconception has its basis in the fact that there is a legal obligation to provide emergency or palliative treatment to a patient who is a patient of record in your practice. There is absolutely no basis in law or in ethical guidelines that supports this misconception as stated. The truth is there are patients who will contribute to your well-being and there are patients who will not contribute to your well-being. If you accept the fact that your obligation is first and foremost to the well-being of your practice and your staff, then you will quickly see it is not your obligation to provide ongoing care to a patient who is a threat to that well-being.

An Example:

I have a client in Indiana whom I was seeing one February. The doctor and the entire staff had just returned from a four-day practice management session that had focused on PR, marketing, and building the practice by caring for the patients. In their morning clearing meeting, they discussed ways they could better serve their patients and reviewed potential problems they might see during the day. In reviewing the schedule, they noted that a patient who was coming in was seriously delinquent and had resisted all attempts by the office staff to reconcile the delinquency. In addition, the patient had no-showed and canceled on numerous occasions and was, generally speaking, an uncooperative patient. In their conversation, the staff agreed the patient would probably no-show or cancel at the last minute. Sure enough, fifteen minutes before the scheduled appointment, the patient called to cancel, saying her car was broken down. In their desire to serve their patients and remembering a suggestion made by someone at that weekend seminar, they decided to send a staff member in the doctor's car to pick up the patient and bring her to the office for the appointment. A little like self-abuse I would say.

Here was a patient who was not interested in contributing to the well-being of the practice; in fact, she had proven she was interested in taking what she could get and contributing nothing back. The staff had decided the patient was uncontrollable; yet rather than recognizing the obvious, they chose to subject themselves to continued abuse and actually went out of their way to keep this abusive patient in the practice.

MYTH #4

Things are different for me. I have been in practice here for 20 years; I am in a small town; all of my patients are my friends; and, therefore, I have to run my practice differently.

Comments:

If this misconception were true, there would be as many different types of practices as there are types of communities or types of personalities in this country. That is simply not the case.

Human beings are human beings anywhere in this country, and they will react predictably in the same situations no matter which community, ethnic background, or religious background they may be from. Your patients will respect an organized, efficiently run practice and will understand and respect business management procedures that make sense. All of the considerations in this misconception are based on the desire to remain comfortable—to remain in your groove or mold—and the perceived discomfort of breaking out of that mold and leaving your "comfort zone."

This misconception, in many ways, can be the most damaging, because it freezes you in position and makes you unwilling to take even the smallest step toward improving your well-being. It leaves you powerless to deal with a patient who chooses not to pay you purely because past history has shown that you will not ask for payment. The belief that your particular practice is special or different invalidates all information from whatever source may be available to you. You could not read a magazine article or listen to a lecture, read a book or listen to a consultant and receive any value from it if you believed that information which is good for others is not necessarily good for you because "your practice is different."

Of all the misconceptions or considerations, this is the most damaging and the most paralyzing to the growth and the well-being of a dental practice.

An Example:

I have a client in a small town in the upper Midwest. When I was hired to consult in his practice, he had been the only dentist in his town and had been in practice over 35 years. He practiced conservatively and was respected and well-loved in the community. In spite of that fact, at the time of my arrival, he was in a weak position in the area of credit management and accounts receivable control. His receivables were triple his monthly gross, his collection rate was in the mid-to-high 80% range, and he was almost buried in delinquency.

Needless to say, the recommendations I made were highly confronting and uncomfortable to the doctor. Initially he rejected many of them. Fortunately for this doctor, within a few months after my consultation, his son graduated from dental school, passed his Boards, and came to practice with his father. The son was receptive to the recommendations I had made and felt they made sense. Over a period of time, he was able to convince his father that my recommendations were appropriate and were not a threat to the health and well-being of the practice. Reluctantly, the senior doctor gave in and allowed the policies and procedures to be implemented universally for all patients in the practice.

Years later this practice has been unable to document the loss of a single patient due to implementation of their new policies. Their receivables are down to 1.6 times monthly gross, and their collection rate has averaged 99%. In addition, the practice grew by well over 50%.

MYTH #5

I cannot count on my staff to do an excellent job of selling dentistry and handling credit management in a manner that is best for my well-being.

Comments:

Occasionally the doctor has surrounded himself with an incompetent and/or uncommitted staff or has a key employee who is incompetent and/or uncommitted. In other cases, the doctor has allowed a close friend or relative to become an employee. Even though the friend or relative has proven unable to handle the job at an adequate level of performance, the relationship has prevented the doctor from making the change necessary for his well-being.

In *most* cases, the doctor has no evidence that his staff is incapable of doing an excellent job; however, his fear of turning loose of authority allows him to believe they cannot do the job. Invariably when a doctor realizes his staff has his well-being as one of their primary considerations, and when he releases the authority to fulfill that responsibility to his staff, the practice will start to accelerate.

In almost every case, a committed patient-relations person or a committed treatment coordinator is able to sell more dentistry than is the doctor. A well-trained staff member is able to make financial arrangements of a higher quality than is the doctor. And there is tremendous evidence that collection activity conducted by doctors on delinquent patients is nearly always a disaster.

An Example:

One of our consultants was recently in an office in the Northeast. Upon her arrival in the office, she found morale to be horrible. Not one employee had been employed there for more than six months. In the position of financial secretary there had been six different employees in the last four years. Not coincidentally, delinquency, receivables, case acceptance and cash flow were completely out of hand. The practice was going downhill.

The doctor had his "reasons and excuses." He talked about how difficult it was to get good staff, how hard it was to find somebody who was committed, and how the one thing he had learned was that if you were going to be successful, you had to do it yourself.

The consultant found that this doctor's attitude toward his staff, and his attitude toward staffing in general, perpetuated his problem. He was constantly looking over his employees' shoulders, checking up on their performance, and questioning their decisions. In the clinic this doctor checked every model that was poured, every impression that was taken, and even the consistency of the cement that was mixed. The staff was unhappy and poorly motivated, and the practice was not doing well. The doctor was frustrated and dissatisfied and suffered from a high degree of stress related to these problems.

The turnaround for this practice came when the doctor finally realized "his way" was not working. We obtained an agreement from the doctor to give his financial secretary absolute and total authority over financial arrangements and collection activity. She did not have to go to him for any procedure or policy implementation in the area of credit management and accounts receivable control, short of actually dismissing a patient from the practice. Allowing his financial secretary this level of responsibility and authority was an extremely difficult decision for him to make, and he required continual support in keeping this agreement.

We were also fortunate because there was an employee who recognized the doctor's weaknesses in this area, and who had the courage to confront him when necessary. She also had the integrity to perform a job to the best of her ability without allowing the doctor, or any other outside factor, to be her "excuse" for lack of performance.

After approximately six months, this doctor looked back to see that he had had a measurable improvement in delinquency, and he had enjoyed the most consistent cash flow of any six-month period in his practice history. In addition, his case acceptance was up, and he had not lost a single patient from the practice. In effect, he learned that a financial secretary — that is, a committed financial secretary with integrity — was able to do a much better job than he could do in the area of patient management and accounts receivable control. Fortunately for this doctor and his practice, he took that lesson to heart and eventually granted additional levels of responsibility, and the authority necessary to go with that responsibility, to other staff members.

Although the problems in this office are not totally resolved today, the practice is in significantly better shape than it has ever been and continues to improve daily. The production per hour worked has gone from $140 to over $250. The staff and the doctor are happy to come to work in the morning, and they leave in the evening with a sense of satisfaction at having had a good day and having done their jobs well. This doctor is starting to learn what quality of life is really like.

MYTH #6

It's okay to accept welfare, capitation, and PPOs to fill in the empty time that I have in my schedule.

Comments:

Sometimes my position on this matter is viewed as a lack of consideration for patients' well-being. I limit this discussion to those doctors who have the same vision for their practices as I do and, again, that is an absolute, impeccable quality of life within the practice. There always has been and always will be a group of doctors who do not share this vision. For that reason, patients who utilize the third party plans such as welfare, capitation, and PPOs will always be served.

There is much evidence of damage being done to a fee-for-service private practice that accepts welfare, capitation, and PPOs, and I believe there is no place for these programs in my clients' practices. Filling "empty space" with welfare, capitation, and PPO patients prevents the doctor and the staff from focusing their energies on filling that space with high-quality, fee-for-service patients—the type of patient who will nurture and support the practice and carry it successfully into the next decade.

An Example:

One of our clients is a three-doctor practice in suburban Chicago that is extremely productive at approximately $180,000 per month. A significant percentage of their patients worked for United Airlines (Chicago is corporate headquarters for United Airlines). They were approached by an organization marketing a capitation plan with which they were encouraged to sign up. Initially these doctors had no interest in the capitation plan, being well aware of the real and potential risks with this type of plan. It was then that the marketing rep for this organization dropped the bombshell. United Airlines had recently signed up with them. The United Airlines employees would be offered the opportunity to sign up with the capitation plan which, in effect, provided them "free" dentistry. The doctors now felt if they did not sign up with the capitation plan, they would risk losing up to 30% of their entire patient load. After a number of meetings, they made the decision to participate with this capitation plan.

I received a phone call from one of the staff on the day this decision was made informing me of the decision. I immediately contacted the doctors directly. After discussion with the doctors, it became clear that they believed their patients, if given the choice of getting dentistry for free via a capitation plan or continuing on their fee-for-service plan, would elect the capitation plan. Since my clients were not participating members, they felt the practice would lose the patients. My clients had no faith in their patients.

It has become clear over the years that quality patients — that is, the patients who will contribute to the well-being of the practice clinically, financially, and spiritually or emotionally — are not interested primarily in the fees for that dentistry. After some significant persuasion, the doctors agreed to temporarily postpone the decision to sign up with the capitation plan while tracking carefully their patients employed by United Airlines.

One month went by without losing a patient, then another month, another, and another. After discussing and evaluating the matter with their administrative staff, they found after six months they had lost less than 3% of their patients employed with United Airlines. Each of these employees had been offered the opportunity of joining the capitation plan, but when they found out that it meant leaving "their doctor" and going to someone else in whom they had no confidence, the majority of patients chose to stay even though it meant that their dental care would require more out-of-pocket expense. This is an excellent example of making a decision based on fear of "what might happen" rather than one based on knowledge.

Another Example:

A similar situation occurred in my home town of Portland. However, it was with welfare.

A client of mine was a caring, compassionate person with an honest desire to serve his fellow man. His receptionist was a Southeast Asian immigrant, and through this employee, the doctor became aware of the plight of a number of immigrant families. Their language and employment skills were weak, and in this particular town, they were underemployed and lived mainly from the benefit of public assistance — welfare. Welfare in Oregon pays a small percent of the case fee and takes a long time to pay the claim.

This doctor had openings in his schedule every week that were going unfilled. Because of his desire to serve these persons who truly needed dental care, he chose to accept them as patients, knowing in advance that he would not collect an appropriate fee for the work. He recognized, however, that these people were basically hard working and honest and typically worked themselves out of the welfare environment and became quality, contributing members of society who would be able to afford appropriate dental care.

The problem was once these patients found out my client accepted welfare patients, they inundated his practice. Prior to accepting welfare, he had three to five open hours a week which he intended to fill with the welfare patients. Now numerous welfare patients were calling for appointments. At the time of my arrival in the office, welfare production made up 12–15 hours per week (50%) of his gross production. Welfare had not only displaced his fee-for-service patients, but since the schedule was filled, there was no incentive for his staff to work hard at attracting fee-for-service private patients to the practice. His welfare practice was growing and the fee-for-service private practice dwindled rapidly. This fact, combined with the fact that he was collecting at about 50 cents on the dollar, was strangling the practice.

Before you jump to conclusions, I want to assure you I am not recommending that you not accept welfare. Any health care professional, no matter what his specialty, can afford to do some charity work. Accepting a certain amount of welfare is not inappropriate as long as the amount of welfare is kept under absolute control. The only effective method of controlling welfare that I have ever seen is to limit the total time per week that you will spend providing dentistry to welfare patients. You have only to determine what percentage of your total productivity you are willing to dedicate to welfare and apply that percentage to your appointment schedule. For instance, if you are willing to do welfare/charity work to 5% of your gross and you schedule 32 hours per week, then 1.6 hours per week could be dedicated to welfare and charity work.

Although I have used welfare as an example, the same rule applies for any charity work or deeply discounted work whether PPOs, discounted direct reimbursement plans, or closed-panel plans.

MYTH #7

I need to conduct my practice defensively, especially in the administrative area of the practice, to avoid potential conflicts with my patients so that they do not become alienated from the practice and speak poorly of me in the community.

Comments:

This misconception is based on one of the most common fears seen throughout the health care field. Doctors fear that if they do anything which will “rock their patient’s boat,” there will be negative repercussions for the practice. They fear patients will leave the practice or will quit referring to the doctor or will speak poorly of the doctor in the community.

I consider this fear “brain damage,” because there is no basis for it in the real world. This fear has caused doctors to refuse to take steps that would enhance the overall well-being of a practice and has actively denigrated the quality of life within a practice.

To overcome this fear requires faith in your staff and their ability to present policies and procedures to your patients in an appropriate manner. It also requires faith in human nature and in the belief that the majority of humans, when faced with reasonable and appropriate rules, regulations, and procedures, will comply with them. Doctors must believe that quality patients appreciate the care they receive from a highly organized and efficient practice that is not at the mercy of the weaker patients.

An Example:

In 1984 we were hired by a doctor in Chicago. I did his consultation personally and found that he had a fine practice, with fairly routine types of problems in the area of credit management and accounts receivable control. One of the recommendations I made was that he charge interest on his open accounts after 60 days from the date of treatment. He accepted virtually all of the recommendations I made, except the one with respect to charging interest.

He felt very few other doctors in his area were charging interest. Since he had been in practice in this community for a long time, he felt his patients would not accept his charging interest. He also felt the negative repercussions on the office would be much greater than any perceived benefit of charging interest.

Nevertheless, in spite of his reservations, he indicated to me that he would start charging interest. When the consultation was finished, I left the practice and wrote my report a few days later, assuming that the doctor would implement each of the recommendations I had made. Six months later, I was asked to come back into the practice to train a new financial secretary. Upon my arrival I found that the office had implemented the majority of my recommendations but had gotten cold feet again when it came to charging interest. As of my arrival, interest was not being charged to their patients. I confronted the doctor with his failure to keep his agreement with me. To keep a long story short, the office started charging interest 30 days later.

Approximately three days after the first interest charges appeared on patients' accounts, I got a phone message from their new financial secretary. The message said simply, "Help" in large block letters. I called the office back, and the comments were, "It's horrible. Patients are leaving the office in droves. The phone has been ringing off the hook for three days. Patients are threatening us. The doctor has decided we must go back to not charging interest." All the fears were coming true.

After filtering through the hysteria, I discovered that this office had, in fact, received 27 phone calls from patients in that three-day period. When the actual conversations were analyzed, most of the calls were coming from patients who were questioning the interest and were not necessarily upset by the interest charge. Of the 27 patients who called, only one had actually indicated that she was going to leave the practice, and at this point, two weeks after the last statements had gone out, they had received no additional calls.

To give you some background, this was a very large practice serving over 2,000 active patients with account balances. The calls they got represented less than 2% of the patients being charged interest. Today, over two years later, they have no evidence that a single patient left the practice. They are still charging interest, and the only phone calls they get are calls from patients with routine questions about their account balance or insurance payments. Charging interest is an accepted policy of the practice, and far from causing problems, is doing what it is intended to do — encouraging patients to make short-term financial arrangements and to keep their payments coming in on time.

Had this practice, which now enjoys extremely low delinquency and an appropriately high counter collection rate, decided to continue to practice defensively, they would not have enjoyed the results that they are enjoying today.

MYTH #8

Patients who do not accept my diagnosis are either uncommitted to their health and well-being or are just shoppers.

Comments:

I have heard this comment many times the past few years, and it never ceases to amaze me that doctors truly believe this. As mentioned earlier, with only a few exceptions, patients who are shoppers are shopping for an experience. If they fail to accept your diagnosis, in most cases it is because your practice has failed to create the type of experience that these patients are seeking. It is more comfortable to believe that a patient who did not accept your diagnosis was uncommitted or a price shopper and, therefore, that he was "wrong," rather than to consider there may be something out of place in the practice that caused this patient not to choose your care.

An Example:

I have a client in orthodontics who was having a serious problem with case acceptance which, at the time of our consultation, was hovering around the 50% range. The doctor was convinced that he had a bunch of uncommitted, "low-test" patients who were only interested in price and not in receiving a quality product. My associate, Jackie Shoemaker, conducted the consultation and had the opportunity on two separate occasions to present a case and make a financial arrangement with new patients. Both of the patients with whom she made financial arrangements had indicated, in one way or another, that they were not necessarily interested in starting orthodontics, but they were only there in one case to "obtain a second opinion," and in the other case to "check the cost of orthodontics."

Often when faced with a presentation such as this, a doctor and/or a staff member would be unwilling to take the same amount of time with that patient that they would take with a patient who indicated from the start that he intended to accept the doctor's diagnosis.

Jackie, however, recognized that patients rarely shop for price; they shop for experience. Communication to you from a patient that he is there to get a price or to get a second opinion is a defense mechanism so he can feel "right" or "justified" at leaving the practice without having accepted the diagnosis. Since Jackie had no "brain damage" on this subject, she focused her energies on communicating effectively with these patients and on selling not just the case, but also the doctor, the practice, the staff, the physical facility, and the quality of the results. In other words, selling the experience.

In both cases, these "shoppers" accepted the diagnosis and scheduled an appointment for the proposed treatment. This generated $5,400 in revenue for the practice and brought two new patients into the practice who otherwise would have been written off as shoppers or persons uncommitted to their health.

Clearly your own personal opinion of and attitude toward the patient is going to affect whether or not he ultimately becomes your patient. If you are going to hold your patients as "shoppers" and "uncommitted to their health," I assure you they will turn out to be just that. Conversely, if your intention is to educate them and to bring them into your practice, you will be successful in that goal, also.

MYTH #9

If I had a computer, everything would be better.

Comments:

The simple fact is that an office can operate very effectively and efficiently using a manual pegboard system, a batch billing service, or an in-house computer system. A computer is not a magic machine with all the answers. If an office is doing no marketing on a manual system, they will do no marketing on a computerized system. If an office is inefficient and unorganized on a manual system, it will be inefficient and unorganized on a computerized system. A computer is nothing more than a tool that helps an office accomplish a specified job. The primary purpose of that tool is to maintain patient accounts, track balances, post treatment, and post payments.

An Example:

I have a client on the Northeast Coast who is a general dentist whose productivity had grown in the past few years to approximately $40,000 a month. He was on a manual pegboard accounting system that was perfectly adequate to serve the accounting needs of the practice. However, since the practice had grown significantly and because of his desire for continued growth, he became intrigued by a computer system that advertised its benefits for marketing.

The computer sales people assured the doctor they had a fine staff training program and excellent follow-up, and that the system would do all of the marketing his practice would ever need for the foreseeable future. In addition, he was told the system was so sophisticated and efficient that he would not need a special treatment coordinator or PR person since the marketing could be done by any existing staff member who could operate the computer.

Slightly over a year later, I was back in the office doing a follow-up consultation, because cash flow had become quite sporadic and delinquency had started to increase. After less than an hour in the office, I was able to trace virtually every problem in the area of credit management directly to the computer program. Although the system had excellent tracking programming and wonderful marketing potential, the system's credit management programming was inhibiting the ability of the office staff to handle credit and collections in an efficient manner. The system would hold no more than a few months of patient history before needing to be purged, making it extremely difficult and time consuming to obtain payment and treatment histories more than six months old. The system had no efficient method of tracking delinquency, and the response time of the system was so slow that the employees responsible for operating the system were spending their time just doing the basics such as posting treatment, posting payments, printing insurance forms, and printing the daily and month-end reports. There was no time left for marketing.

In addition, there was a tremendous sense of dissatisfaction and frustration among the staff and the doctor at having spent $40,000 for a computer system that, in retrospect, did absolutely nothing to enhance the overall well-being of the practice or the quality of life within that practice.

The moral of this story is that no matter what size practice you operate, it is possible to operate efficiently and profitably without a computer. If you choose to purchase a computer, purchase it for the right reasons. *Do not* purchase the computer to "fix" anything, because it won't do that. If you are already efficient and organized, the computer can help you become more so. If you are not efficient and organized, stay away from a computer until you become efficient and organized.

MYTH #10

High receivables are good for the practice; they provide a financial cushion. It's okay if I didn't collect all of my production this month; at least it's on the books and we'll collect it eventually.

Comments:

A study of value economics by the University of Chicago a number of years ago showed that professional receivables paid at the time of treatment are worth 100 cents on the dollar. If they are left on the books for even 90 days, their value declines to 87 cents on the dollar, and the decline continues the longer they are left on the books. The fact is, every time dental care is provided and not paid for at the time of treatment, there is some risk that the practice will never be paid at all.

If your average collection rate is 90% today and has been 90% for a number of months, when will you ever collect the 10% of production that is not being collected every month? Even if you collect 100% of production for a number of months, you would not collect any of the money that is currently on the books. In order to collect what is in receivables, you would have to collect more than 100% over a very long period of time. How many doctors are ever successful in doing that? It usually only happens when a practice suffers a significant decline in productivity, which, of course, has a negative impact on the practice.

My question is, if you can collect 100% of your production each month while maintaining low receivables and enjoying high productivity, why would it be considered appropriate to maintain high receivables? The difference is one of technology — the technology that you will learn in this book.

An Example:

I recently had the opportunity of appraising the receivables for an organization involved in selling dental practices. The selling doctor had always had what he considered to be a "successful" practice. He had been in practice in a relatively large town in Texas for many years and was looking forward to his retirement. In addition to selling his practice, including his equipment, his patients' records and charts, he chose to sell his accounts receivable which totaled slightly over $250,000. He had advised the practice broker he would be able to get 90% of face value for his receivables, and he felt $225,000 was a fair price. I was brought in to appraise the receivables. After a thorough analysis of the patients' accounts representing those receivables, an appraisal was established at approximately $100,000.

To say the selling doctor was shocked and disappointed is an understatement. He had operated for years in the belief that money which is put on the books will eventually be collected. He had collections each month which were always relatively close to his production. When he had a burst of productivity and a corresponding increase in receivables every few months, he did not worry because it was considered "normal." When his financial secretary came to him periodically with accounts which were uncollectible, he suggested she continue to work them as best she could. Uncollectible accounts were allowed to clutter his receivables.

When I reviewed the receivables, I found that 70% of all of the accounts that were on the books had been there more than 60 days. Less than 25% of the accounts were current.

Although this doctor did sell his practice, he chose not to sell the receivables for such a depressed price, and he hired an administrative person to work as a collector. Ultimately almost $100,000 was written off as uncollectible. Approximately $150,000 was collected over an 18-month period of time at a collection cost of between $25,000 and $30,000. Clearly the "cushion" that this doctor felt he had did not exist.

MYTH #11

Granting credit does increase patient satisfaction and case acceptance but results in sporadic cash flow, increased delinquency, and decreased net income. Being restrictive in granting credit gives me good cash flow and very little delinquency but creates a significant problem with patient satisfaction, case acceptance, and referral rates. Therefore, if I take a middle-of-the-road approach, I can have the best of both worlds.

Comments:

The problem here is the lack of technology. History has shown that a middle-of-the-road policy can save you from some of the problems associated with granting credit to weak patients and can allow patients to accept care who would not have otherwise. The evidence that a middle-of-the road policy is working would be low delinquency, low receivables, high and consistent cash flow, high net income, and high case acceptance. However, I rarely see this performance from a middle-of-the-road policy, because adequate technology has not been put in place. A middle-of-the-road policy will not enhance the ability of your patients to accept your diagnosis and will not stop "deadbeat" patients from radically damaging the quality of your practice life.

An Example:

The best example that I could give is that of your own practice. If you are reading this book, very likely you have what we have described as a "middle-of-the-road" policy in the area of credit management and accounts receivable control. Has this policy allowed you to be delinquency free? Do 100% of your patients accept the diagnosis you have made?

Myth #12

The existing figures are acceptable (e.g., case acceptance, collection percentage, receivables ratio, delinquency ratio, aged receivables percentage, counter collections percentage, and production per hour).

Comments:

My experience with this thought is that very few doctors would actually turn down an improvement in performance figures if that improvement could be had with little or no effort, or little or no discomfort. My position, of course, is that accepting weak performance purely to maintain your comfort zone is unacceptable and unnecessary. Why should you be willing to accept 25% delinquency if 20% were possible and if, by reaching that 20%, the overall well-being of the practice would be enhanced? Why would you accept a 95% collection rate if a 98% collection rate were possible and if, by collecting 98%, the well-being of the practice would be enhanced?

This actually relates back to the earlier misconception, "the way things are is the way they will continue to be," and most often comes from resignation to existing figures and not *satisfaction* with the figures.

An Example:

In 1984 I was in Texas giving a lecture to a local dental society. As part of a lecture I routinely will list the types of performance figures that are realistic and acceptable goals for an office; for instance, a 98% collection rate, a 2–3% delinquency rate, etc. One of the recommendations I had made in this presentation was that I felt a general dental practice's accounts receivable should not exceed 1.5 to 1.75 times average monthly production.

At the end of the day a doctor came up to me with questions regarding that particular recommendation. As it turned out, he was the head of a multi-doctor practice that was producing over $300,000 per month, and he had total accounts receivable in excess of $1 million. His collection rate had always been what to him was acceptable, and his delinquency was under relative control. Until the time he heard my presentation, he had never felt the need for improvement. In his opinion, his receivables were in line, especially given the fact that articles he had read in various dental magazines had indicated that receivables of two to three times gross production were appropriate, and even his own accountant had indicated that his receivables were "in good shape." What he thought he heard from me was that his receivables were not healthy, and that is not at all the point that I was trying to make.

My purpose in suggesting that accounts receivable be at 1.5 times production (in this office, $450,000 instead of $1,000,000) was not to imply he was a failure because of his receivables, or that he would be a success if he got them to $450,000. I explained to this doctor that if he maintained receivables at $450,000 instead of $1,000,000, that additional $550,000 could be used to enhance his well-being or the well-being of his practice. This is just simple economics. He could pay off debt, he could fund pension plans, he could fund staff incentive plans, etc.

Faced with this new information that it was possible to collect well and, at the same time, have lower receivables, he looked at areas in his practice that he had previously ignored, such as the areas of credit management and accounts receivable control. He decided a consultation was appropriate. Having learned new techniques of controlling receivables, this doctor and his associates are today producing approximately $400,000 per month. In spite of this significant practice growth, they have been successful in reducing total accounts receivable to slightly under $800,000. Certainly the practice is in better financial health today than a few years ago, because they learned that something better was possible.

CHAPTER 2

RECEIVABLES MANAGEMENT MYTHS: MISCONCEPTIONS ABOUT THE NUTS AND BOLTS FACTS BEHIND SUCCESSFUL COLLECTIONS

INTRODUCTION

Most doctors consider collection activity to be a necessary evil. They consider the value of collection activity to be limited to the additional revenue created by the collection of a past-due account. Often when delineating job descriptions, they will separate the "collections" job from that of the financial secretary's position. They fail to recognize the close relationship between collections and patient management. In locating a person to do collections, they will look for someone with past collections experience, to the extent of requesting collection agency or finance company collections experience.

If the primary goal in conducting collection activity is simply to collect a past-due account, then an office can probably obtain reasonable results by utilizing a "collector." However, I believe the role of the collector — or more importantly, the reasons for conducting collection activity at all — is on a higher plane than merely collecting a few extra dollars.

What is the real damage done to a practice by having a delinquent patient on the books? Is the true damage the $100 or $200 that the practice is missing? If you take the time to analyze your delinquent accounts, you realize the practice is being damaged to a far greater degree than the loss of funds. As has been mentioned previously, a disproportionately large share of the patient-related problems in the practice (no-shows, cancellations, weak referrals, malpractice claims, and poor home care) will come from the small percentage of past-due accounts.

Why is it that delinquent patients cause such a high percentage of non-money related problems? It is because these delinquent patients are in a negative relationship with the practice. It is fairly easy for us to relate to this type of situation, because from time to time each of us fails to keep an agreement that we have made. Think back to the last time that you failed to keep a formal agreement that you made with somebody. It may have been an agreement to pay a debt, an agreement to meet somebody at a particular place, any agreement whatsoever. When you failed to keep that agreement, especially if there was no good cause, a certain amount of guilt was involved, and perhaps even a certain amount of fear at being confronted. Depending on the level of guilt or the fear of confrontation, you may have avoided the person with whom you made that agreement. This is exactly what is going on in your office whenever you have a delinquent patient.

Therefore, the value of maintaining patients' accounts in a current status and of reducing delinquency is not the additional revenue that is generated but rather the improvement in relationship between the practice and the patient. This is a simple concept that should be easy to understand. For whom would you rather do a complex, time-consuming technical procedure? A patient who is current and with whom you have a positive relationship, or a delinquent patient whom you do not enjoy being in the same room with? The role of your financial secretary — of your "collector," if you will — is to work with your delinquent patients, to nurture and support them so that you will renew a positive, mutually fulfilling agreement.

The role of the collector is not to collect a past due account, but to resolve the problem. The problem, of course, is the delinquency and the negative relationship associated with that delinquency. Resolution of the problem can come from one of three steps:

1. Payment in full of the delinquent amount. Obviously this would be your first choice and is a solution which should be sought wherever appropriate for the patient.

2. Establishing or, more often, re-establishing a formal financial agreement. This may be a new agreement in the event one did not already exist or, in the event that a previous financial arrangement was broken, it may be a recommitment to another financial agreement. This recommitment may be to the original agreement or to a new agreement calling for increased monthly payments, decreased monthly payments, or increased length of financial arrangement. The most important aspect is a formal agreement that the patient can keep — an agreement that is realistic for you and for the patient. By realistic for you, I mean a monthly payment and a length of financial arrangement that will amortize the debt over a realistic period of time. For instance, a $20-a-month financial arrangement is not realistic nor reasonable for a $500 account balance. Remember, we are not interested in band-aiding the problem. We are interested in resolving the problem so that it does not become a negative issue for the practice.

3. The answer may be to write the account off as uncollectible and dismiss the patient from the practice. This step needs to be looked on as a realistic alternative. It is not meant to be facetious or sarcastic. Occasionally you will make mistakes; you will grant credit to a patient who does not have the ability to pay you or, more commonly, a patient who does not have the willingness to pay. Once your financial secretary has determined that she is unable to resolve the problem by collecting the past-due amount, the only resolution to the problem will be to write the account off as uncollectible and dismiss the patient from the practice. You will remember from our earlier discussion, that the problem with delinquency is a patient who is in a negative relationship with the practice. Anything that eliminates that particular situation is problem resolution. So clearly, writing an account off and dismissing a patient resolves the problem.

Occasionally, there will be a situation where you are unwilling to dismiss a patient. There could be clinical reasons where dismissal of a patient is not advised, but more often the reasons will be personal. For instance, the patient may be a friend of yours. When you are faced with this situation and your financial secretary has determined that the account is uncollectible — that is, uncollectible in a reasonable manner — then the account must be written off the books. You have the option of continuing to keep the patient in the practice *on a no-charge basis.* In other words, recognizing that this patient does not have the ability or perhaps willingness to pay for his or her care, and also accepting the fact that you are not willing to dismiss the patient, future care will be done at no charge. *Do not* make the serious mistake of keeping the account on the books, and *do not* make the mistake of agreeing to treat the patient on a payment-in-full basis. This is a gross disservice to your patient and, in the long run, you will get caught again and will end up writing off even more. In any event, this is certainly no way to reach your vision if your vision includes quality of life within the practice.

MYTH #1

I should not start collection activity too soon because I may offend my patients.

Comments:

This again is a misconception of what is healthy for the well-being of a practice and is based on an unfounded belief that prompt collection activity will alienate your patients. There is no evidence to support this misconception.

Previous collection activity which may have resulted in negative patient comment is unlikely to have resulted from collection activity conducted too soon but rather from inappropriate collection activity. More likely, and this is opposite of what most practices have believed in the past, the negative communication and the problems were caused by waiting too long to conduct collection activity.

The earlier you can conduct quality collection activity, the better will be your results. Conversely, the longer you wait to conduct collection activity, the poorer will be your results.

The reasoning behind these statements can best be demonstrated by an example.

An Example:

Most of us have been at a checkout stand at a grocery store after having filled a basket with our week's supply of groceries. If, while our groceries are being checked and totaled, we note that a 25-cent candy bar was overlooked by the checker and had been put in our sack by the box boy, we would very likely instruct the checker to please ring up the missed item. We would not do that because of our legal obligation. There was no sheriff standing behind us with his gun drawn threatening to arrest us if we did not pay 25 cents for the item. So, if it was not our legal obligation motivating us to pay, what was it? Clearly, it was our moral obligation. In other words, we felt the right thing to do was to pay for the candy bar even though we had "gotten away with" not paying for it.

What if, however, we did not notice the candy bar and we started for home. During the trip home the traffic was horrible, it was raining and our windshield wipers quit working. Upon arrival at home, a tire went flat in the driveway. A few minutes later, while putting away the groceries in our kitchen cupboards, we discovered the candy bar that had not been paid for. The legal obligation to pay for that candy bar remains and has not changed in the 30 minutes since we left the grocery store. However, how many of us would repair the flat tire, repair the windshield wiper, get back in our car and fight the traffic to return to the store and pay for the 25-cent candy bar? I suspect very few of us would make that choice. Something has happened. The legal obligation to pay has not changed. What has changed is how we feel about paying for it. Our felt moral obligation has changed. In this particular case, time, distance, and inconvenience have reduced our desire to keep our legal obligation.

As time goes on, how we feel about keeping an agreement is diminished to one degree or another. It is for this reason that collection activity must be conducted the moment you determine an account is past due or that a patient has failed to keep an agreement.

The risk of alienating or upsetting a patient is far greater when you are conducting serious collection activity on an account that is two, three, or more payments past due, than when conducting low-key, casual collection activity with a patient who is 10 to 20 days past due.

MYTH #2

I can establish rules, policies, and procedures for control of delinquency in my office; however, I have to allow for exceptions to the rules for my friends, my neighbors, members of my church, and other people that are special to me.

Comments:

I suppose the truth of this misconception depends on your vision for your practice. If you believe this myth, I ask you to look at your aged or delinquent receivables and interview your administrative staff. Upon investigation, you will see that patients for whom you have established "special" rules or patients to whom you have allowed "special" treatment will invariably cause problems for your staff and ultimately problems for the practice as a whole.

Overcoming this myth requires some courage and faith: courage to be at risk and faith in a well-trained administrative staff to handle collection activity in an appropriate manner. It requires faith in your friends, your neighbors, members of your church, and other people special to you, that they will recognize you have a business to operate. Further, they will recognize an agreement will be made on how debts will be paid, that the agreement must be kept, and every effort will be made to obtain a recommitment when the agreement is broken. You must take a pragmatic view of collection activity. The damage done to your practice by having friends and relatives past due is far greater than the damage done by having quality collection activity conducted with them once they become delinquent.

My recommendation in this respect is simple: Do not charge your patients fees that you do not fully intend to collect. Once a fee has been charged out, there should be no obstacle that would prevent a well-trained administrative staff person from working the delinquent account to an acceptable conclusion.

The same policy should be in place with respect to financial arrangements. Each patient needs to have a financial arrangement on major treatment plans. The fact that a patient may be a friend, relative, or church member should have no bearing on that policy. If you are unwilling to have an administrative staff person make an appropriate financial arrangement with a patient, then the patient should not be charged for the treatment in the first place.

An Example:

I have a client in a coastal town of Southern California. When I arrived in his office to conduct the initial phase of our consultation, I found that over 50% of the accounts in his office were 30 days or more past due. His financial secretary advised me that she had been prevented by the doctor from conducting formal financial arrangements with these patients. She was also prevented from conducting collection activity on this group of patients when they fell behind.

As it turned out, the doctor was a bishop in his church, and the patients who made up the majority of the delinquency were members of the same church. The doctor felt that since these were good, honest people, they would pay him if they could. If they did not pay, that was evidence they were having financial hardship and were, in fact, unable to pay. He further felt that if the office were to conduct collection activity, it would damage his reputation as a leader in the church and in the community.

I obtained credit reports on a significant percentage of these delinquent patients and found that in over 90% of the cases these patients had responsible jobs. Many were white-collar executives with impeccable credit. These were people who had never missed a payment to anybody except this particular doctor.

There is an old adage that the doctor always gets paid last. In my experience, this is only true because the doctor historically has always asked last. Human beings being human beings, we will very often get away with exactly what we are allowed to get away with. This was certainly the case with the delinquent patients in this particular practice. This doctor ultimately was incapable of overcoming his resistance to handling his church members in an appropriate, business-like manner. His financial secretary left in frustration and over the years has been replaced with a number of others. Today, six years after that initial consultation, the practice has failed to grow and continues to suffer with serious delinquency.

MYTH #3

I need to use collection agencies, small claims courts, and attorneys to help collect from my "deadbeat" patients. I can judge my financial secretary's performance by how many delinquent accounts she is able to collect.

Comments:

This is an extremely common myth and the resolution is one of the most difficult for doctors to accept. When you have worked hard and provided a service for your patients and your patients fail to pay for that service, it is very often considered a "slap in the face," a personal attack on the doctor, and, at the very least, a blow to the doctor's ego. The problem is magnified if the patient with the uncollectible account has the ability to pay and is consciously choosing not to do so.

Set your ego aside and recognize that there is no long-term value to the practice of having your ego satisfied by "getting back" at your patients by using collection agencies, small claims courts, or attorneys. You will remember from my discussion earlier that the purpose of collection activity is to resolve the delinquency problem. The problem is not that the account is past due; the problem is not that you have failed to collect a few dollars. The problem is that you have patients in a negative relationship with the practice. While patients are in a negative relationship, they cannot or will not contribute to the well-being of the practice. They will not refer their friends and relatives to your practice, they will not show up for future appointments, they will not be in a position to accept additional diagnoses.

If this is the true nature of the problem, what is to be gained by using collection agencies, attorneys, and small claims court? Outside sources of collection will do nothing to enhance your relationship with these patients. If anything, they will only make it worse. If you consider your time and the time of your financial secretary, you will realize the time spent working on uncollectible accounts by outside sources will not be cost effective. It is important to work a delinquent account quickly, before the patient's relationship with the practice has had an opportunity to be severely damaged. If, while working on old uncollectible accounts, even a single quality patient is allowed to fall out of relationship with the practice, then the damage exceeds any potential benefit gained from collecting a few dollars from a "deadwood" account.

It takes courage to live this philosophy and to not send an account to a collection agency, small claims court, or an attorney, especially when that patient is one who has personally offended you by lack of payment. Certainly this is a situation where it is necessary to be uncomfortable in order to reach your vision.

There are additional tools which are available to you to deal with patients such as these, which will be described in following chapters.

An Example:

I was in a new client's office recently, and this practice never wrote off an account. This office routinely sent accounts to collection agencies or, when the balances were large, to a collection attorney. Their accounts receivable, therefore, was astronomical.

Due to the sheer volume of accounts, there was no way of separating those which were collectible from those which were uncollectible.

I evaluated this office's accounts and found that in the last five years the return from the collection agencies had been only 10.5% of the total accounts sent to the agency. Since the agreement with the agency required them to return to the collection agency 50% of all funds collected, their net return was less than six cents on every dollar. I would think the emotional freedom of not having to deal with thousands of dollars of uncollectible accounts on your books each month would make up for this weak return in funds.

They also had used small claims court and a collection attorney on a number of accounts. They were pleased to advise me that they had been successful in obtaining judgments against almost every patient that they had sued. They had judgments on over 20 patients. In obtaining these judgments, they had also incurred a fairly significant amount of unreimbursed court costs and filing fees. I was unable to track even a single case where they had been paid in full as a result of obtaining those small claims court judgments. Clearly these are situations where this office was winning the battle and losing the war.

Today this office has written off all of their uncollectible accounts. They no longer utilize the services of collection agencies or any other outside collection source. At the very least, their mental health has been enhanced and their financial health has not been damaged.

MYTH #4

I do not need to send statements to a patient unless his account is past due. Sending statements upsets my patients and by not sending statements, I save a significant amount of hassle and expense for postage.

Comments:

Although it's true that sending statements does increase office overhead, the tangible and intangible benefits far outweigh this slight increase in expense. My position is that sending a statement is a courtesy and will go a long way toward increasing patient satisfaction with the practice. Anytime there are more satisfied patients, every other aspect of their relationship with the practice improves as well; specifically, referrals from these patients.

There is no evidence among the thousands of offices that have switched from not sending statements to sending statements that patients are alienated by receiving a statement of their account.

Other benefits to sending statements, more tangible than increased patient satisfaction, are decreased delinquency and a measurable increase in monthly cash flow.

Most negative comments from patients about sending statements have to do with the change in policy and not the fact that the statements were received. Historically, many health care practices have sent statements only to patients who were past due. When the office changes the policy and sends statements to patients every month without first informing their patients, there is likely to be negative communication. The patient assumes you consider him to be delinquent. Clearly the solution to this minor problem is to educate your patients in advance that statements are being sent as a courtesy.

If you were to go to Sears, Montgomery Ward or J. C. Penney and purchase a major appliance, they would put you on a sales contract. This is an account which allows you to make monthly payments over a fixed period of time. Even though your account may have been paid ahead and had no monthly payment due, you still received a monthly statement. Most major banking institutions in the United States realized long ago that monthly statements reduced delinquency and increased cash flow. Therefore, they eliminated or cut back the use of payment books and payment coupons in favor of a monthly statement.

It is important to differentiate between a "statement" and a "bill." A bill is a document, the receipt of which indicates that a payment or perhaps the balance is "due" such as a utility "bill" that you may receive each month in your home or a "bill" from your attorney for services rendered. A statement, on the other hand, is information regarding the history of your account for the previous 30 days. A well-written statement shows any treatment or charges posted to the account for the previous 30 days, any payments made and will differentiate between insurance payments and patient's payments. As an example, a patient may receive a statement that shows he received $100 worth of care and paid $20 (his portion not covered by insurance), leaving a balance of $80, all of which will be paid by insurance. In this situation the statement does not indicate that you expect the balance to be paid by the patient. You are merely telling him what has happened on his account over the previous 30 days. If, on the other hand, the balance remaining on the account is owed by the patient, the statement may be determined to be a bill which in this situation, it is. If, because you sent monthly statements, one or two patients paid you who would have otherwise neglected to do so, the cost of sending your statements would already be recovered.

An Example:

I have a general dentist as a client who does a fairly substantial amount of major treatment plans, including orthodontics. Patients receiving major care, especially orthodontics, were most often put on extended payment plans with payment arrangements ranging from two months to as many as thirty months. When I did this doctor's original consultation, his office was on a "billing service," which sent statements to patients with an account balance. They had recently converted to a "sophisticated" computer system. As a way of justifying the cost of the computer, the salesman advised them they could avoid the expense of sending statements. This particular computer system would print payment coupons which were "much better than statements." In addition, the computer would automatically send statements (bills) to patients if the monthly payment agreement should become past due.

As a result of an alarming increase in delinquency, I was asked to come back into the office for a follow-up visit. I arrived in the office approximately eight months following his conversion to his new computer system. At that time I found that over 30% of his patients were 30 days or more past due. After evaluating the situation in the office, it became clear that although he had always had delinquency in his office, the rate of delinquency increased as soon as they converted to their new computer system. The fact that he was no longer sending statements to his patients, except when they were past due, was contributing to the problem. I had this client send a letter to his patients and advise them as follows: "As a courtesy to our patients, we will be sending a statement of your account each and every month. The statement does not necessarily indicate that a payment is due; it is designed to inform you of the most recent history on your account. Please call our office if you have any questions." A minor change in the computer format eliminated coupon books and sent monthly statements to these patients from that date forward. With virtually no other change in his practice, there was an immediate decrease in 30-day delinquency of over 25% and, of course, a corresponding increase in cash flow.

CONCLUSION

Finally, all these thoughts, misconceptions and ideas based on past performance, assumptions and guesswork, all this "brain damage," will not be cleared up unless you have a vision for your practice and your life within the practice.

It is important that each of us establish a vision of how we would like our life to be at some point in the future. A vision is something beyond the level of a goal. It's intangible; something you can't quite grasp; a picture, perhaps, in your mind. Webster defines "vision" as "something seen by other than normal sight; a mental image."

A vision is a 14-year-old on his first rock climb deciding to climb Mt. Everest. A vision is a small boy shooting his first rabbit deciding to hunt an imperial elk. A vision is a small girl with a paper airplane deciding to one day pilot the Concorde. All of these visions will require some amount of discomfort if they are to be reached.

Imagine for a moment what life would be like if each patient in your practice was so thrilled with the experience of being your patient that he actively referred his friends and neighbors to you. Imagine for a moment what it would be like if you rarely had a patient who canceled his appointment at the last minute or no-showed. Imagine what it would be like if every patient accepted immediately whatever care you diagnosed. Imagine what it would be like if every patient always paid for his health care in an appropriate manner, and you had a delinquency rate of 0%. These are visions of how your practice could be in the future.

Most of us have a commitment to our goals or to our visions if they have been established, but that commitment is limited. That limit is our comfort zone. Most of us will do whatever it takes to reach our vision as long as we are able to remain within our zone of comfort. For instance, a doctor might allow his financial secretary to write collection letters to a past-due patient, but what happens when that past-due patient is the doctor's next door neighbor and his wife's very close friend? All of a sudden exceptions are made. The commitment to the vision is reduced because of the need to be comfortable. Commitment has been defined as, "the willingness to be as uncomfortable as it takes to reach the desired result."

Robert Pante was heard to say recently at a lecture in Phoenix, Arizona, "You cannot reach your visions within your current comfort zone." This is an important statement for us to understand. It is human nature to want to be comfortable. Most of us spend our lives striving for physical and emotional comforts, and we will do almost anything to stay comfortable. Our vision of our practice is the ultimate practice, and yet we are told that we cannot become supremely comfortable and maintain our comfort on the journey to that vision. Unfortunately, this is sometimes true. I would like to demonstrate this point by telling you a true story.

I have a very close friend who happens to be a general dentist. We live very close to one another, we often see each other socially, we have vacationed in Europe together, and our wives have been close friends for many years. One of the things I know about this man is that he is absolutely and unconditionally committed to his quality of life within his personal life and, in particular, within his dental practice.

In mid-1987 a woman came into his practice with two young children. She was a new patient, and her request was for a prophy, exam, and x-rays for her children. She completed the necessary paperwork, and the exams and prophies were performed. Since this doctor, in addition to being my friend, is also a client, his administrative staff evaluated the mother's personal situation as evidenced by the patient history form and obtained a credit bureau report while the children were being treated in the operatories. A review of the patient history form disclosed that the family had just moved into our city from out of town and that the husband had a weak employment background. A credit bureau report indicated that they had filed bankruptcy recently and, since the bankruptcy, had run up additional bills which they had left unpaid. Two of the bills which had been left unpaid were small doctor bills.

At the completion of the appointment, the financial secretary asked the mother to pay in full for the treatment her children received that day. This sum was around $90. The mother made a small payment on the debt and promised to pay the balance within a few days. At this same time, she made an appointment to have a couple of small fillings done on one of the children.

The date the payment had been promised came and went, and the balance was still unpaid on the date the mother and child arrived back in the office four weeks later.

Prior to the time the child was seated, the mother was asked to pay the $50 past-due balance and to pay for the treatment that was going to be rendered that day. The mother apologized profusely for allowing the account to fall behind and apologized again when she advised the financial secretary that she was unable to pay for that day's charges as well. The financial secretary then advised the mother that they would be unable to treat her child that day and would, in fact, be unable to provide further dental care until such time as the account was paid in full. Further care would be provided on a cash-only basis.

Given this mother's history with this practice as well as the evidence that the mother was a person not to be trusted to handle debt in an appropriate manner, this practice handled the party in an exemplary fashion according to the guidelines we would have recommended. The thing that makes this situation unusual is that the patient was my sister, and the children involved were my niece and nephew. This is an excellent example of commitment to a vision—a commitment even to the point of extreme discomfort.

I am sure when the financial secretary was faced with dismissing a patient who was the sister of one of the doctor's close friends she had some second thoughts. When she checked with the doctor and he supported her in making the best decision for the well-being of the practice, his commitment became very apparent.

Once the vision is established, once you have a clear picture of where you want to be, then you will find a road that opens up to lead you to that vision. As you take each step, cross each hurdle or pass each milepost, as you measure your progress and see your results, you will experience a tremendous level of satisfaction and accomplishment. Just as you celebrated your first paying patient, your first $1,000 day, or your first $25,000 month, so also will you celebrate along the path to this new vision—your first week without a no-show or cancellation, your first month with 100% case acceptance, your first year with 100% collections, your first day with no delinquency.

Once you start to taste the fruits of your labors, your past fears and considerations will melt away, and you will accelerate along the path to your vision in a geometric progression that will bring about a state-of-the-art practice in a short period of time.

You must have a vision, you must have a belief that it is possible to reach that vision, and you must have a commitment to be as uncomfortable as it takes to reach your vision.

SECTION II:

NUTS AND BOLTS

CHAPTER 3

UNDERSTANDING PATIENT MANAGEMENT

The first step in my process is patient management.

As you are aware by now, it is not going to be possible to reach the vision that you have for your practice unless you recognize and accept that there are patients in this world who cannot or will not contribute to your personal well-being or the well-being of your practice. This is not good or bad; we don't have to make judgments about it. It is what is true.

Different people in this world have different levels of integrity; they are in different socio-economic situations; they have different levels of motivation concerning health care; and each of your patients will contribute to the well-being of the health care practice to a different degree. Fortunately, it is possible with a high level of accuracy to quantify or qualify patients; that is, to categorize patients (or potential patients) so you can quickly and easily identify a patient's credit risk and his potential for contributing to the well-being of your practice.

Categorization: A Risk Assessment Tool

Often the doctor or his staff have negative feelings associated with the thought of "categorizing" patients. So before I proceed, I would like to emphasize one point: you will *never* be quantifying, qualifying, or categorizing patients as to their value as a human being. All of your patients and prospective patients will be treated with love and respect and with absolute consideration for their needs.

However, you must recognize that you are in the *business* of dentistry. If that business is going to be successful, you need to recognize your obligation — not only to yourself but to your patients — to identify the patients who will contribute to you in a manner equal to the level at which you are willing to contribute to them. And it is necessary for your well-being that you nurture and support those patients to the best of your abilities. Further, you must identify those patients who will not or cannot contribute to your well-being. The pragmatic health care practitioner will recognize that this type of patient must be brought into the practice only under a strictly controlled environment. The environment we are speaking of is the environment surrounding finances, money, and the fee for the health care that has been or is about to be provided.

When your financial secretary is evaluating a new patient who has just arrived in your office, she is, in effect, acting as a loan officer or credit manager. The financial secretary must make a decision as to the level of credit risk or financial risk that your practice may have with that patient. She must use that decision to determine what type of financial arrangement is appropriate for that particular patient.

Would it be appropriate, for instance, for you to provide a financial arrangement of one-third down and the balance over two or three months for a patient who is 23 years old, single, working part-time pumping gas at a gas station and who has a credit report that indicates he has been written off as uncollectible by numerous creditors, including previous health care providers? The answer is obvious.

However, the opposite side of this example is much more important. Would you, for instance, be willing to lose a patient who was a permanent, long-term resident of your area with 20 years as a homeowner and 20 years on his job with perfect, impeccable credit just because he could not afford or, perhaps, did not choose to pay the one-third down that your office policy requires? Again, the answer is obvious.

Both of these situations occur daily throughout the country. Solid, substantial citizens of the community routinely do not accept care that has been diagnosed or go to other dentists because their dentist has a restrictive credit policy. The practice with the aggressive credit policy is living with significant amounts of stress and frustration and losing large amounts of money because their aggressive credit policy was not sufficient to protect them from the patient who is unable or unwilling to pay them appropriately for their health care.

The key then, is to abandon any practice philosophy or practice policy requiring all patients be treated the same, with respect to their finances. You must recognize that different patients have different levels of integrity and different levels of motivation or priorities concerning dental care. Therefore, the financial policy of the practice must be structured to fit each individual patient. For instance, with one patient, it may be appropriate that you require payment in full in advance of treatment. With another patient, it may be appropriate that you allow no down payment and 12 months to pay the balance. Again, the situation will change with each individual patient.

If you are going to have a policy that allows you to be flexible, you must have a system that identifies the risk level of each patient so that you will not grant liberal financial arrangements to risky patients, nor will you be too restrictive with solid, mature patients.

Credit Management: The ABC's of Risk Analysis

To this end, I recommend that each patient coming into the practice be grouped into credit risk categories. For purposes of this book, I am going to be using "A," "B," and "C." There are actually seven categories of credit risk that I will be discussing ranging from "A+" to "C" and which I will describe later. But for now, "A," "B," and "C" will suffice. The "A," "B," and "C" are not technically important; you can call them "X," "Y," and "Z"; "1," "2," and "3";

"green," "yellow," and "red"—whatever. What I am recommending is a system of identifying credit risk level for your patients. Remember this ABC classification system is to allow you to determine the type of financial arrangement appropriate for a particular patient. It will in no way affect your diagnosis.

A "C" patient is a patient who "cannot" or "will not" pay for health care in an appropriate manner. For instance, a patient who is unemployed and has no source of revenue other than unemployment insurance or welfare is a "C" patient. You are not saying that this patient could not afford to pay you $40 for a prophy, but this is the type of patient who could not afford to pay for the normal range of dental care. This is a "cannot." Most "C" patients are those who "will not" pay appropriately for dental care. These are patients with credit records (credit reports) that indicate they have not paid their debts to other creditors.

A "B" patient is a patient who is either young or unstable; or a "B" patient can be a very mature and stable person who happens to have a weak credit record. An example of the "B" patient would be the young, single person working part time as a gas station attendant that I previously mentioned. This is certainly not the type of person that you would want to give unlimited credit to. So, you would classify him as a "B" patient. An "A" patient is a patient who is mature and stable and who has a good credit record. This is the type of patient you would like to surround yourself with. This is the type of patient upon whom you would like to build your practice. And this is the type of patient you must be willing to grant whatever reasonable level of credit is necessary to encourage him to accept the diagnosis that you have made.

There are variations on these basic ratings. For instance, in addition to the "A" patient there is also the "A+" and the "A−" patient. The same is also true in the "B" category; there is a "B+" and a "B−." There is no "C+" or "C−," however.

A Deeper Look at Each Category

The "C" Patient. A "C" patient is a "C" and must be handled on a payment-in-advance basis. In general dentistry, and in all specialties other than orthodontics, a "C" patient should be given absolutely no credit. If *special* care is taken to ensure that insurance will pay a portion of the "C" patient's bill and if you are certain this insurance company accepts your assignment of benefits, accept the patient's insurance, stipulating that the patient's fee not covered by insurance be paid in advance. For the orthodontic patient in the "C" credit risk category, the most liberal financial arrangement should be a down payment of 50% of the case fee and the balance paid over a period of time not exceeding one-half the estimated time for completion of treatment.

You may think that this is a highly restrictive financial arrangement, that your "C" patients would be unlikely to accept the arrangement, and that you would lose patients as a result. My response is that I hope that *is* the result. Remember that a "C" patient is a patient who *cannot* or *will not* pay you appropriately for your health care. If you have an absolute, unshakable commitment to your vision and if your vision includes being delinquency free and having a high quality of life, then there is no place in that vision for treating this "C" type patient.

But, you might ask, what about the poor, downtrodden patient who, through no fault of his or her own, is financially incapable of paying for health care? Who will serve their needs? The answer is: you, should you so desire. However, the work must be done at absolutely *no charge.* If you have clearly determined that a patient is in a situation where he is incapable of paying appropriately for the health care that has been diagnosed and if you have a situation that makes it necessary that you treat that patient anyway, then, again, the treatment must be provided at no charge.

Many doctors like to subscribe to the "spaghetti" principle; that is, throw it against the wall and see what sticks! Unfortunately, that doesn't work in credit management, especially not if you have a financial secretary who is committed to your well-being. And especially not if you have a financial secretary who has been given goals that include maintaining delinquency and receivables at appropriate levels. How could you, in good faith, 1) put a patient on the books whom you have already determined is incapable of paying you appropriately for the health care that you have diagnosed, and 2) charge him for that health care anyway. Can your financial secretary agree to be held accountable to maintain delinquency at appropriate levels, to maintain receivables at appropriate levels, and to maintain your monthly collection rates at appropriate levels if you are going to put patients on the books who are financially uncontrollable? I would certainly hope not. The answer, with these patients, is not to treat them (my first choice) or, in special situations, to treat them free of charge. In my opinion, there is no middle ground in this respect.

The "B" Patient. The "B" patient is not a deadbeat but rather is a patient you would probably like to have in the practice. However, his circumstances at this time are such that he cannot be granted unlimited credit. "B" patients should be handled by requiring a 50% down payment with the balance of the fee to be paid over a period of time not exceeding three months. This financial arrangement is appropriate for general dentists and all specialties other than orthodontics. For orthodontics a "B" patient should be required to pay 25–30% of the gross case fee as a down payment with the balance of the case fee to be paid over a period of time not exceeding 75% of the estimated time for completion of treatment; for instance, 18 months on a standard 24-month orthodontic case.

As with "C" patients, you will perhaps lose a patient over this financial arrangement. It may not be a problem to lose a patient in the "C" category because of financial arrangements, but now you are talking about "B" patients — patients you would love to have in the practice. When this comes up, you may find yourself having second thoughts. When I review my clients' figures and when I do follow-up visits in my clients' offices, I find that it is the "B" patients with whom they are the least consistent, and with whom they get into the most trouble. Quite often there is an emotional attachment to keeping these "B" patients in the practice. Remember, however, that the patient was categorized as a "B" because he was young, unstable, or in a credit situation which prohibited extension of liberal credit.

Again, reviewing your commitment to your vision, you will recognize that bringing a patient into the practice in an out-of-control situation will very likely prevent you from reaching your goals. Dealing with "B" patients is very often where practices become "prostitutes." They sell out to maintain their comfort level. Here's an example:

Mrs. Jones has been in the practice for 10 years and she has always paid her bill in the past. However, it has taken a significant amount of time and effort to collect it. A $400 crown took nine months to collect, requiring multiple collection letters and phone calls, and resulting in uncomfortable feelings among the staff. Yet, here she presents herself again. How are you going to respond? She is a "B" patient by virtue of the fact that she did not pay on the last dental care she received. Being a "B" patient she must have a 50% down payment and a formal financial arrangement that calls for the balance to be paid over two or, at the most, three months. Yet this is the same person who has been in the practice for 10 years. Are you willing to abandon your "comfort zone" and let your financial secretary handle Mrs. Jones appropriately? Or are you going to "prostitute" yourself — sell out — to remain comfortable and recreate the collection problem you recently got rid of? (Hint: Your financial secretary should use good verbal skills and request an appropriate down payment and an appropriate monthly payment from this patient. Then be absolutely willing to lose the patient if she is incapable or unwilling to pay in the manner that you desire.)

The "A" Patient. An "A" patient is a patient who is mature and stable and is not the type of patient who is likely to become a credit problem for your office, assuming you have normal and routine credit and collection policies in place. Fortunately, "A" patients make up the vast majority of all patients in your practice, and they are the patients with whom a restrictive credit policy would be entirely inappropriate. Your financial secretary must use good verbal skills to encourage your patients to pay quickly and efficiently; but, 1) if this "A" patient happens to be in a temporary financial situation which makes a particular down payment inappropriate or perhaps uncomfortable, and 2) if his situation makes the required monthly payment inappropriate for him, then your primary focus of selling the case and serving this patient requires that you be liberal in your financial arrangements. Make whatever financial arrangement is appropriate to encourage this patient to accept your diagnosis. If that means no down payment and six months to pay on $1,000 of dentistry, then that is acceptable. Even on an orthodontic case, if that means no down payment and 30 months to pay (even on a 24-month treatment plan), then that would be appropriate. Would you really be willing to lose this good, solid, mature, stable patient (who has never missed a payment to anybody) because of your restrictive credit policies? I hope not. With good office financial policies, with appropriate financial incentives, and, most importantly, with fine verbal skills, you will rarely find yourself in a position where it is necessary to give a patient long-term financial arrangements. But doing so should certainly be within the realm of possibility with patients who have been determined to be of high quality.

In addition to the ABC system, there is a second tier of categories which help evaluate a patient as a credit risk. This second tier is known as the 3 Cs: character, capacity, and conditions. It is the evaluation of these 3 Cs that allows your financial secretary to make the ABC decision.

Credit Management: The 3 Cs

The financial secretary of a health care practice routinely makes credit decisions beyond the level of authority of the small bank manager or small finance company manager in America today. I see financial secretaries making credit decisions on $3,000 and $4,000 orthodontic cases; $5,000 and $10,000 oral surgery cases; and general dental cases that can run in the $10,000 to $15,000 range. If you were to apply for a loan at the average bank branch or consumer finance company in the amount of $10,000, those branch managers would be required to check with a senior manager at a separate location for approval for that dollar amount. Yet these managers are highly trained credit management executives who have been in credit management for many years. Clearly there must be training for the financial secretary if she is going to make these serious decisions.

To understand credit management, the first thing to remember is that a bank officer or loan office manager does not make a profit unless he finds a way to approve a loan. Quite often bank managers, as well as financial secretaries in health care offices, are deemed the "bad guys." People seem to think they try to find a way to turn down the loan. Actually the opposite is true—a good bank manager or financial secretary will try to find any way possible to approve the loan or to approve the patient for a particular financial arrangement. You can't make money in the *business* of dentistry unless you are approving the financial arrangements for the care that you are diagnosing. With the overhead of the average dental office in this country today, neither can you make money in the business of dentistry if you grant credit to a person who is not going to pay or who is not going to pay appropriately. Neither can you afford to be right 90% of the time and wrong 10% of the time. The average dental office will have to do the same amount of dentistry six to ten times and be paid in full, just to break even, when one account is uncollectible.

Evaluating the level of your patient's credit risk is a simple process, and it is done the same way a major New York bank makes the decision to make a billion dollar loan to an American corporation. Every bank manager, every loan officer manager, and every credit manager looks at the applicant and evaluates what are called the three "Cs" of credit: character, capacity, and conditions.

Character. Character has two subcategories: integrity and stability. Character is actually somewhat intangible, but a credit manager can paint a picture of the applicant and deduce, with accuracy, the character of his applicant by determining his level of stability and his level of integrity or honesty. Has this applicant been around the area a long time, and does he pay his bills? You can see this in your own life experience. Generally speaking, people 50 years old are more stable (from the credit management point of view) than people who are 20 years old. People who are married are more stable, generally speaking again, than people who are single, divorced, or separated. People who are homeowners tend to more stable than those who are apartment dwellers. People with 20 years on the job tend to be more stable than people with 10 days on the job. People who are corporate presidents tend to be more stable than people who are underemployed as agricultural workers. This is not meant to display prejudices against any particular class of people, any particular living situation, or any particular work environment. It is important, as I have stressed before, that you recognize that you are in the *business* of dentistry. Look at your own experience. Review the last 10 accounts that you wrote off as uncollectible. How many of them were 45-year-old adults with 20 years on the job and 20 years in your area? How many of them were married and in an otherwise stable environment? What you will very likely find is that of those you wrote off, the majority were people in an unstable situation. They may, for instance, have been young, they may have been divorced or separated, or they may have had a short time on the job or a short time in your area. This is not to suggest that you should be rude, discourteous, uncaring, uncompassionate, or inconsiderate of the patients who are 20, or those with only six months on the job, or those who are recently divorced or separated, or those living in apartments. I am merely stating that different levels of stability affect a person's willingness and/or ability to pay appropriately for health care. This is just common sense.

The first part of evaluating a person's character is to look at his stability, then look at his level of integrity. In other words, how has this patient or potential patient handled his debts with other creditors? Are you more willing to grant credit to a patient with a history of extensive credit and who has never missed a payment or to a patient who has been written off as uncollectible by numerous physicians and dentists and who has had his car and other merchandise repossessed?

This first category of the three "Cs"—character—is by far the most important. A person with a high level of integrity and honesty will keep his agreements even though it may be difficult in certain situations for him to do so.

Most human beings are basically honest and will keep their agreements. If you take the time to identify patients with a high level of integrity, you will find these people will contribute to your well-being. In turn, you can contribute to their well-being, even during periods of your patient's unemployment or other times of turmoil that may come throughout your relationship.

Capacity. The second of the three "Cs" is capacity. Very simply, that is your patient's financial ability to pay you. Does this patient have the funds or the future income to be able to afford the dentistry that you would like to present? Putting too much emphasis on this can be dangerous because the average financial secretary or the average doctor is not capable of determining a patient's capacity or ability to pay a particular bill. The average history form completed by your patients does not give you enough information to make that decision. Neither should you use a patient history form that requests that type of information. It is not necessary for the type of work you are doing. You should, however, be aware that it is possible for a health care practice to put a patient into a highly untenable financial situation. Dentistry can generate some very high fees, and I am sure that everyone reading this book can identify the patient who for years was an excellent patient as long as he only received prophies, exams, or other forms of routine care. Then, when $3,000 or $4,000 worth of work was done, he became a serious collection problem. Some attention must be paid to a patient's capacity to pay for health care. Your particular decision would be based on: Does my patient have a reasonably good job with at least an adequate income to cover basic needs and routine dentistry?

Conditions. The third and final category to be used in evaluating your patients is the community conditions in which you and your patient live and work. This is a very intangible category to evaluate. While the first category, character, and the second category, capacity, will be evaluated with all new patients, the third category, community conditions, will not. For instance, you may read in the morning paper that a particular employer in your area is going to lay off 80% of their workers, or is going to close and move out of your area. If, on that same day a new patient comes into the office who is employed by this company, the astute financial secretary would explore the patient's situation through a verbal interview to determine whether or not this plant closure is going to affect this patient's ability or willingness to pay for the dental care that you diagnose.

Credit Risk Evaluation: A Realistic Perspective

When I give lectures on this particular topic, I routinely ask the audience what percentage of their new patients they believe fall into the various categories. It is not at all uncommon for financial secretaries and doctors to believe that the vast majority of their existing and new patients fall into the "B" and "C" categories. Nothing could be further from the truth.

I have been fortunate enough to visit the offices of doctors in all fifty states and throughout Canada as well. I have been in dental offices in the urban areas of New York City, Los Angeles, Chicago, and Detroit as well as small western towns like Bend, Oregon; Bozeman, Montana; and Fargo, North Dakota. Whether the practice is located deep in an urban environment, in an oil town in the Southwest, in Stone Mountain, Georgia, or in Manitoba, Canada, I have found that 85–90% of new patients clearly fall into the "A" patient category. Consider how many patients would walk into a dental practice who are underemployed, unstable, immature, or have serious credit problems? The answer is, at most, 10–15%.

If you accept that 85–90%, maybe 95–98% in some offices, of all patients are "As" and if you also accept that "A" patients, being mature and stable, are very likely to keep their agreements and pay for their dental care in an appropriate manner (assuming they have made an agreement to do so), your previously established credit policies may start to seem overly aggressive.

You might ask: if 85–90% of all my new patients are "As," how is it that I have so much delinquency or why when I used to grant credit more liberally than I do now did I suffer so many financial difficulties? The answer is that people are human and will do exactly what they are allowed to get away with.

If a patient has dental work done for $1,200, and the office does not establish a financial arrangement (which includes a particular down payment and a particular monthly payment due on a particular date in time), it is likely that even though he is able to afford this dental care, he will not pay appropriately. (When the office does not conduct collection activity appropriately, the problem increases. There will be more on this later in the book.)

Summary

1. It is appropriate to evaluate your patients and to place them into various categories of credit risk in much the same way a bank, consumer finance or credit union manager does when faced with a loan applicant.

2. Once a patient has been "categorized" into certain levels of credit risk, you can use that information to determine the type of financial arrangement that is appropriate for the practice and for that particular patient. You can be more liberal in your financial arrangements with the 85-90% of your patients who fall into the high quality category, thereby enabling them to accept your best diagnosis and to be satisfied in their relationship with your practice.

3. In addition, you can identify the patients who represent a moderate level of risk for your practice and utilize a financial arrangement which will enable them to accept the care you have diagnosed.

4. Finally, you can identify the small minority of your patients who are unlikely to contribute to the well-being of your practice. You can restrict finances to such a degree that they will either choose not to be your patient or choose to pay in a manner that will cease to cause future problems.

Evaluating and categorizing your patients and handling these patients in a manner commensurate with their level of credit risk will enhance the well-being of your practice by increasing case acceptance significantly and by reducing receivables and delinquency. This puts you well on your way to reaching your "vision."

In the next chapters, I will address the mechanical tools that will assist you in evaluating your patients and making the ABC credit decisions.

CHAPTER 4

CREDIT EVALUATION TOOLS

If you are going to have a policy of evaluating your patients — their stability, or, perhaps, their lack of stability — then your office must have tools that help you make that credit evaluation decision responsibly.

Before I discuss what the tools are, I would like to discuss what they are not. They primarily are not instinct or feelings or opinions based on personal bias rather than facts. Historically, decisions on granting credit or decisions on methods of handling patients have been based on how patients looked, talked, acted, or walked. I have even seen credit decisions based on how the patients dressed or what type of cars they drove. In addition, decisions were made based on the new patient's referral source or whether or not that patient knew somebody who was already in the practice or, perhaps, was a friend or relative of the doctor or some other staff member in the practice. Obviously, none of these criteria have any bearing on the patient's true level of risk to the practice. Yet many dental practices use the very criteria I have mentioned with predictable results.

Patient History Form

Recognizing that you are acting as a loan officer or credit manager, you must use the same tools that are used by loan officers and credit managers. Those tools start with a credit application. In a health care practice this document is called a "Patient History Form."

The forms that are used in health care practices are very poorly designed — at least poorly designed to do the job of evaluating the party responsible for paying for the health care. Their primary purpose has been to give basic information in order to "bill" the patients. Rarely have these forms been designed to make a credit decision.

Stop for a moment and review the patient history form that your office is currently using. You may find that your existing form requests a certain amount of information on the "patient" and very little information on the person who is responsible for paying for the dental care you are about to provide. (In some extreme cases the only question asked about the party responsible to pay for health care is that person's name.) If the responsible party is a person different from the patient, you often are left without an address or any other information to help you make a credit decision.

Before you run out and ask your friendly banker for a copy of his credit application, you need to recognize that you are not a lending institution but rather a professional health care office. You need to balance your desire to learn about your patients and their responsible parties with a certain sense of professionalism. You must avoid the appearance of commercialization. And you must not become too intrusive. You should not request information about the patient that you cannot or will not specifically use in making your decision regarding the patient. For example, some patient history forms ask for the patient's or responsible party's driver's license number. When I ask why this information is being requested, the staff has absolutely no idea and says the information has never been used, but that "We have always asked for it." Once in a while, an especially astute financial secretary will say, "We use driver's license information to help us collect if a patient writes an NSF check." However, it is extremely rare that a patient has become delinquent and the staff has been able to collect because they had a driver's license number.

When designing a patient history form, the general rule should be: 1) ask only for information that will allow you to make a credit decision, and 2) ask only for information that will not be deemed intrusive. There may be instances where some patients may consider certain requested information to be intrusive. However, if that information is necessary to make your credit decision, then good verbal skills can be used to overcome the patient's discomfort. Another thing to remember is that your patient's interpretation of what is intrusive may be different from what a credit manager, a practical business manager, or the financial secretary in a dental office may consider intrusive.

I have included a sample patient history form (see Page 47) which can be used as a basic guideline for designing your own. As long as you are requesting the needed information, the format or layout can be varied. The information may be compressed on a half-page form or expanded to cover a two-page form. It can be incorporated or not incorporated with a health history. As long as adequate information is obtained on the person responsible for payment of the health care, the layout is unimportant.

No matter how well a form is designed, no matter what information is requested, and no matter how much attention you intend to give to the evaluation of the document, a patient history form is useless unless it is completed to the last detail. For instance, what good is it to ask a patient how long he has been employed if your patient leaves that information blank? If your patient's name is Edwin P. Jones, a patient history form indicating that his name is Ed Jones (no legal first name, no middle initial) will be of limited value.

If you were to pull the charts of your 10 newest patients (if yours is the typical dental office), I imagine you would find only three or four were complete — at least by my standards. Good verbal skills in this area are going to be imperative.

Success in obtaining complete and accurate information is based on two approaches: carefully interviewing the patient immediately following completion of the patient history form, or filling out the form for the patient. Remember, a few moments after completion of this form your financial secretary is going to be reviewing it and making a credit decision that could very well affect whether or not the patient becomes a member of your practice. When faced with inaccurate or incomplete information, the natural tendency among credit managers and financial secretaries is to be conservative and to make an effort to protect themselves. Obviously, being too conservative with a patient with whom you do not need to be conservative could very well cost you a quality patient. And trying to get a patient history form completed after it initially has been filled out incompletely is more difficult and more uncomfortable for the patient and the involved staff member.

Consider the possible progression of your credit decision. If this patient is a quality patient (which is very likely), you are willing to make an "A" decision. The patient then accepts your diagnosis and you provide quality health care that serves the patient. This patient is then likely to refer family, friends, and even acquaintances to your practice. Under this scenario, your credit decision may very well have an economic impact of tens of thousands of dollars on your practice.

Do not take completion of the patient history form lightly. It does make a difference whether the patient has a middle initial or not. It does make a difference whether the patient has a nickname or not. It does make a difference whether you obtain a residential address or mailing address.

You will note in the example (Fig. 4–1), I have separated patient information and responsible party information. Certainly if your patient is not the financially responsible party, you will need very little information other than health history on the patient. Remember, also, that at this stage you are trying to determine the level of your responsible party's stability.

1. Marital Status: Remember that marital status affects stability. It is appropriate that you request information on the responsible party's marital status.

2. Residence and Mailing Address: Be sure that you have a complete residential address as well as a mailing address if they are different. A post office box is certainly acceptable as a mailing address, but it cannot help you determine the neighborhood in which your patient lives or whether they are living in an apartment or a house.

3. How Long at This Address: How long your patient has been at the residential address will assist in determining his stability, and that information should be requested. If your patient has resided at a particular address less than three years, I recommend that you obtain his previous address. Did he just move to your area from out of town? Has he been in your area his entire life? Again, what is his level of stability?

Patient Information

A B C

Date ____________

Patient's Name ____________ (Last / First / Middle)

Address ____________ (Street / City / State / Zip)

Home Phone ____________ Birthdate ____________ Social Security # ____________

If patient is a minor, give parent's or guardian's name ____________

Whom may we thank for referring you to our office? ____________

Responsible Party Information

Name ____________ (Last / First / Middle / Marital Status)

Residence ____________ (Street / City / State / Zip)

Mailing Address ____________ (Street / City / State / Zip)

How long at this address ____________ Home Phone ____________ Work Phone ____________

Previous Address (if less than 3 yrs.) ____________ (Street / City / State / Zip)

Social Security # ____________ Birthdate ____________ Relationship to Patient ____________

Employer ____________ Occupation ____________ No. Years Employed ______

Spouse's Name ____________ (Last / First / Middle) Relationship to Patient ____________

Employer ____________ Occupation ____________ No. Years Employed ______

Social Security # ____________ Birthdate ____________ Work Phone ____________

Insurance Information

Insured's Name ____________ Insured's Soc. Sec. # ____________

Insurance Company ____________ Group No. ____________ Local No. ____________

Insurance Co. Address ____________

Do you have dual coverage? Yes ☐ No ☐ If yes:

Insured's Name ____________ Insured's Soc. Sec. # ____________

Insurance Co. ____________ Group No. ____________ Local No. ____________

Insurance Co. Address ____________

Insured's Employer ____________

Emergency Information

Name of nearest relative not living with you ____________

Complete Address ____________

Phone ____________

I understand that where appropriate, credit bureau reports may be obtained.

Signature (Parent's signature if minor) ____________

Updates (date & initial) ____________ ____________ ____________ ____________ ____________

CONFIDENTIAL (for record and pretreatment evaluation)

Fig. 4–1

4. Social Security #: You should request a Social Security number. It will help when it comes time to get a credit report which I will discuss shortly.

5. Birthdate: Certainly birthdate is necessary because age will be a significant factor in your credit decision.

6. Employer: Employer is the next item on the form. Request the actual name of the employer for whom the responsible party is currently working. This may seem obvious, but I routinely see answers in this area such as "Union Local 26." It is extremely rare that a patient works *for* a union; it is more common that he works *through* a union. If your financial secretary is going to make an intelligent credit decision, she needs to know whom the responsible party is working for today!

7. Occupation: The next question to ask is the nature of his employment. Is he a welder, a carpenter, a physician, a bank manager, a gas station attendant, a grocery store clerk? If he works for the local bank, whether he is the president or the most recently hired part-time teller will have impact on the credit decision.

8. No. of Years Employed: Of course, how long the responsible party has been employed by that particular employer will affect your credit decision.

9. Spouse's Information: Spouse's name, employer, occupation, and phone number are equally desirable information.

10. Insurance Information: I will be discussing acceptance of insurance assignment later in this book. For now it is sufficient to say that insurance information identified in the sample form will be imperative to your future dealings with this patient.

11. Emergency Information: This information may be viewed as optional. However, there have been a number of situations where that information has been helpful in locating the new address for a patient who has disappeared, or in getting a message to a patient otherwise inaccessible. In addition it is excellent information in the event of a medical emergency with your patient while he is in your office.

12. Credit Report Disclaimer: Since you are going to be obtaining credit reports on your patients, the statement, "I understand that where appropriate, credit bureau reports may be obtained," can be useful.

13. Finally, be certain to obtain the signature of the person completing the form.

The information presented in this document is not meant to be all-inclusive. It is, however, the document that is used most commonly by our clients throughout the country. Certainly there is additional information you can request which may help your staff member make a decision. However, this form does a good job of balancing the information in order to be as unintrusive as possible while, at the same time, getting sufficient information to make a quality decision.

As I mentioned earlier, a patient history form that is well designed is useless if not well completed. Moreover, a well-completed, well-designed patient history form is useless unless a responsible staff member (usually the financial secretary) takes the time to thoroughly review the form, line by line, and uses the information to determine the level of stability and, therefore, the level of risk.

A Review of Sample Patient History Forms

Please review the following patient history forms as you would if you were a loan officer deciding whether or not to lend this patient $1,000 of your own personal money. Once you have thoroughly reviewed these forms and once you have a solid feeling of the level of credit risk, make a note of the credit rating you consider appropriate for this patient. Remember that the credit ratings will range from "A+" to "C." With each patient history form, I will give the correct rating for the patient and the reasons for that rating. Make your own analysis before you read mine.

As a review: 1) "A" patients are mature, solid, stable people; 2) "B" patients are patients who are less mature or less stable; 3) "C" patients are patients who are clearly incapable of paying for the dental care that you diagnose or who would be incapable of paying for that dental care in an appropriate manner.

Remember that you can use pluses and minuses with your "A" patients as well as with your "B" patients but not with "C" patients. A "C" is just a "C." An "A+" patient would be extremely stable—the cream of the crop, so to speak. A "B−" patient would be an extremely unstable person who represents a high credit risk for you, but is a patient for whom you do not have physical evidence that they cannot pay for health care. These ratings will become clearer to you as you go through the attached forms.

Analysis of Fig. 4–2. You have a married, adult couple in their mid-to-late thirties. They have 12 years at the same residence. Mr. Simmons has 10 years on the job and Mrs. Simmons is an executive with a local bank.

Decision: Risk Category Rating: "A+"

Patient Information

A B C

Date 9-10-87

Patient's Name Simmons (Last) Pamela (First) Elizabeth (Middle)

Address 175 Pioneer Trail (Street) Honolulu (City) Hawaii (State) 97000 (Zip)

Home Phone 555-8690 Birthdate 4/1/77 Social Security # n/a

If patient is a minor, give parent's or guardian's name Tom and Marie Simmons

Whom may we thank for referring you to our office? Dr. Jim Smith

Responsible Party Information

Name Simmons (Last) Thomas (First) Edward (Middle) M (Marital Status)

Residence 175 Pioneer Trail (Street) Honolulu (City) Hawaii (State) 97000 (Zip)

Mailing Address same (Street) (City) (State) (Zip)

How long at this address 12 years Home Phone 555-8690 Work Phone 555-4900

Previous Address (if less than 3 yrs.) n/a (Street) (City) (State) (Zip)

Social Security # 297-00-0000 Birthdate 5/18/51 Relationship to Patient Father

Employer Simmons Fine Furniture Occupation owner No. Years Employed 10

Spouse's Name Simmons (Last) Marie (First) Elizabeth (Middle) Relationship to Patient Mother

Employer 1st National Bank Occupation Vice President No. Years Employed 8

Social Security # 297-00-0001 Birthdate 9/23/52 Work Phone 555-5251

Insurance Information

Insured's Name Thomas Simmons Insured's Soc. Sec. # 297-00-0000

Insurance Company Aetna Insurance Group No. BA20705 Local No. --

Insurance Co. Address 1000 First Street, Los Angeles, CA 90039

Do you have dual coverage? Yes ☐ No ☒ If yes:

Insured's Name ______ Insured's Soc. Sec. # ______

Insurance Co. ______ Group No. ______ Local No. ______

Insurance Co. Address ______

Insured's Employer ______

Emergency Information

Name of nearest relative not living with you Kathy Smiecik

Complete Address 245 S. 57 Avenue, Honolulu, Hawaii 97000

Phone 555-7439

I understand that where appropriate, credit bureau reports may be obtained.

Signature (Parent's signature if minor) Thomas Simmons

Updates (date & initial) ______ ______ ______ ______ ______

CONFIDENTIAL (for record and pretreatment evaluation)
Zuelke & Associates 1986

Fig. 4–2

Comments:

1. Your patients will rarely be more qualified. Both people have good jobs. They have been at their current residence for an extended period of time. They are married, and their age supports their stability. Therefore, excellent stability is shown.

2. You may have rated Tom Simmons an "A" or "A – ". That is natural because you will tend to protect yourself and your practice until you become familiar and comfortable with this evaluation technology.

3. This form is an excellent example of how a completed patient history form should look. Notice there is not a single blank on the form which is not filled in, even to the extent of "n/a" being indicated in two of the blanks.

Analysis of Fig. 4–3. Bruce is single. He is in his 20's. He has lived two years at his current residence. Bruce's previous address is in the same city. He is a lifetime resident of Indiana and graduated from Indiana State University. He has six months on the job. Bruce has dental insurance.

Decision: Risk Category Rating: "B + "

Comments:

1. Note: the role of the financial secretary is to find a responsible way to grant credit to prospective patients. In Bruce's case an astute financial secretary, upon examination of the patient history form, realized that unless some stability is determined, no credit can be requested. (This is a mark of a staff member who is truly dedicated to the well-being of the practice.)

2. The financial secretary obtained additional information on Bruce — lifetime resident of Indiana, graduate of Indiana State University. This helped in making the proper credit evaluation.

3. Bruce's age, his short time on the job, and his marital status (single) make him a somewhat unstable risk.

4. However, he does indicate some stability in that he finished college and has been working in the same industry for at least 2 1/2 years. Also, he has lived at his current residence for two years and his previous residence was in the same city.

5. These facts taken together make me want to rate Bruce a "B + ". I do not want to be overly generous with granting him credit, but neither do I want to be overly restrictive.

Patient Information

A B C

Date 9-10-87

Patient's Name White (Last) Bruce (First) Edward (Middle)

Address 245 Haylard Way (Street) Indianapolis (City) Indiana (State) 46200 (Zip)

Home Phone 555-7849 Birthdate 10-11-65 Social Security # 297-48-0789

If patient is a minor, give parent's or guardian's name ---

Whom may we thank for referring you to our office? Sharon Sybil

Responsible Party Information

Has always lived in Indiana. Attended Indiana State U.

Name See above (Last / First / Middle) S (Marital Status)

Residence See above (Street / City / State / Zip)

Mailing Address Same (Street / City / State / Zip)

How long at this address 2 years Home Phone 555-7849 Work Phone 555-2783

Previous Address (if less than 3 yrs.) 258 N. 54 St. (Street), Indianapolis (City), Indiana (State) 46200 (Zip)

Social Security # See above Birthdate See above Relationship to Patient self

Employer Cub Foods Occupation Checker No. Years Employed 6 mos

Spouse's Name n/a (Last / First / Middle) *Previously worked 2 yrs at Safeway* Relationship to Patient

Employer n/a Occupation No. Years Employed

Social Security # n/a Birthdate n/a Work Phone n/a

Insurance Information

Insured's Name Bruce White Insured's Soc. Sec. # 297-48-0789

Insurance Company Aetna Group No. ZZ4085 Local No. n/a

Insurance Co. Address 1000 E. Ninth Avenue, Indianapolis, IN 46200

Do you have dual coverage? Yes ☐ No ☒ If yes:

Insured's Name n/a Insured's Soc. Sec. # n/a

Insurance Co. n/a Group No. n/a Local No. n/a

Insurance Co. Address n/a

Insured's Employer n/a

Emergency Information

Name of nearest relative not living with you Karen Dimeon

Complete Address 8974 Meadow Lane Indianapolis, IN 46200

Phone 555-2931

I understand that where appropriate, credit bureau reports may be obtained.

Signature (Parent's signature if minor) *Bruce White*

Updates (date & initial)

CONFIDENTIAL (for record and pretreatment evaluation)
Zuelke & Associates 1986

Fig. 4–3

6. When evaluating a prospective patient as a credit risk, you must take into account all the information on the patient history form. Each pertinent piece of information about the responsible party then becomes a positive or negative factor in the granting of credit. Remember: you cannot make snap judgments on the basis of one or two pieces of information. You must use all of the information to make your decision. Every piece of information will reflect on every other piece.

Analysis of Fig. 4–4. Robert is in his early 20's. He is single. He lives in an apartment. He has been at this address a short time. His previous address is out of town. He is a gas station attendant with a very short time on the job.

Decision: Risk Category Rating: "B–"

Comments:

1. Robert is single, lives in an apartment, has recently moved to town, and has been on the job a very short period of time. These are all negative factors.

2. Robert's stability is significantly less than that of Bruce on page 52, though their age and current job status is similar. Therefore, we must downgrade Robert appropriately.

3. However, there is no information on the patient history form which indicates that Robert would not be able to pay for the treatment given him, so he cannot be rated as a "C."

Analysis of Fig. 4–5. Margaret is married. She is living in an apartment. She has lived there two months. She has no phone. She is in her 20's. She is not gainfully employed, and her husband is in jail.

Decision: Risk Category Rating: "C"

Comments:

1. Margaret is married, which is positive. However, she lives in an apartment, has lived there for only two months, is currently unemployed, and her husband is in jail—all negatives. This person is highly unstable.

2. The negatives in Margaret's case overwhelmingly outweigh the positives. Therefore, her rating can only be a "C."

3. This is a good time to recall that the ABC credit rating system does not vote on whether or not Margaret is a good person. It will not affect your diagnosis with the patient. It simply indicates how your financial secretary should handle financial transactions with this person. And in Margaret's case that would be on a cash-only basis.

Patient Information

A B C

Date 9-1-87

Patient's Name Roberts (Last) Robert (First) W. (Middle)

Address 1065 N. W. Third St., Apt. 101 (Street) Eugene (City) OR (State) 97501 (Zip)

Home Phone 555-9915 Birthdate 12-21-65 Social Security # 408-00-7642

If patient is a minor, give parent's or guardian's name ________

Whom may we thank for referring you to our office? Yellow Pages

Responsible Party Information

Name Roberts (Last) Robert (First) W. (Middle) S (Marital Status)

Residence 1065 N. W. Third St., #101 (Street) Eugene (City) OR (State) 97501 (Zip)

Mailing Address same (Street) ____ (City) ____ (State) ____ (Zip)

How long at this address 6 mos. Home Phone 555-9915 Work Phone 555-2004

Previous Address (if less than 3 yrs.) 204 Elm, #B (Street) Corvallis, (City) OR (State) 97330 (Zip)

Social Security # 408-00-7642 Birthdate 12-21-65 Relationship to Patient self

Employer Bob's Chevron Occupation Attendant No. Years Employed 2 mos

Spouse's Name None (Last) ____ (First) ____ (Middle) Relationship to Patient ____

Employer ____ Occupation ____ No. Years Employed ____

Social Security # ____ Birthdate ____ Work Phone ____

Insurance Information

Insured's Name No insurance Insured's Soc. Sec. # ____

Insurance Company ____ Group No. ____ Local No. ____

Insurance Co. Address ____

Do you have dual coverage? Yes ☐ No ☐ If yes:

Insured's Name ____ Insured's Soc. Sec. # ____

Insurance Co. ____ Group No. ____ Local No. ____

Insurance Co. Address ____

Insured's Employer ____

Emergency Information

Name of nearest relative not living with you Mrs. Ruth Roberts

Complete Address 956 Grant St., Corvallis, OR 97330

Phone 555-0125

I understand that where appropriate, credit bureau reports may be obtained.

Signature (Parent's signature if minor) ____

Updates (date & initial) ____ ____ ____ ____ ____

CONFIDENTIAL (for record and pretreatment evaluation)

Fig. 4–4

Patient Information

A B C

Date 9-15-87

Patient's Name Martin (Last) (Maggie) Margaret (First) J. (Middle)

Address 604 S. W. Lexington, Apt. C (Street) Los Angeles, (City) CA (State) 40859 (Zip)

Home Phone none Birthdate 3/7/68 Social Security # 503-00-8723

If patient is a minor, give parent's or guardian's name

Whom may we thank for referring you to our office? phone book

Responsible Party Information

Name Martin (Last) Margaret (First) J. (Middle) M (Marital Status)

Residence 604 S. W. Lexington, Apt. C (Street) Los Angeles, (City) CA (State) 40859 (Zip)

Mailing Address same (Street) (City) (State) (Zip)

How long at this address 2 mos Home Phone no phone Work Phone none

Previous Address (if less than 3 yrs.) 901 Maple (Street) Los Angeles (City) CA (State) 40859 (Zip)

Social Security # 503-00-8723 Birthdate 3/7/68 Relationship to Patient self

Employer none Occupation babysit for sister No. Years Employed 2 wks

Spouse's Name Martin (Last) Joseph (First) R. (Middle) Relationship to Patient husband

Employer none; he is in jail Occupation carpenter No. Years Employed

Social Security # Birthdate Work Phone

Insurance Information

Insured's Name no insurance Insured's Soc. Sec. #

Insurance Company Group No. Local No.

Insurance Co. Address

Do you have dual coverage? Yes ☐ No ☐ If yes:

Insured's Name Insured's Soc. Sec. #

Insurance Co. Group No. Local No.

Insurance Co. Address

Insured's Employer

Emergency Information

Name of nearest relative not living with you Pansy Mitchell

Complete Address 703 Oak Street, Fullerton, CA 40621

Phone 555-7724

I understand that where appropriate, credit bureau reports may be obtained.

Signature (Parent's signature if minor) Margaret Martin

Updates (date & initial)

CONFIDENTIAL (for record and pretreatment evaluation)

Fig. 4–5

4. Also, remember that there is an exception to handling C patients on a cash-only basis. That exception is: if the patient cannot pay for your treatment on a cash-only basis and you, the doctor, want to treat the patient. Then you can do so. But, you must do so at NO CHARGE. Do not succumb to the "spaghetti principle." Either get paid in full, do not do the work, or do it free of charge with patients like Margaret Martin.

Analysis of Fig. 4–6. Tom is married. He has lived one year at his current residence. He is in the military. He has been in the Navy three years. He is an officer, and he is a pilot. He is 24.

Decision: Risk Category Rating: "A – "

Comments:

1. Being married is a positive factor. Also, since Tom is an officer and a pilot, you can assume that he has a college degree and is a highly responsible and trustworthy individual. These are all positive factors.

2. Because Tom is in the military you can also assume that he may be transferred regularly. This is a negative in terms of stability.

3. Although Tom is relatively young and could be transferred at any time, he is also a fairly mature and responsible person. Therefore, a stable credit rating is appropriate. However, you do not want to grant him unlimited credit. The negatives in his case are still a factor to be concerned with.

Analysis of Fig. 4–7. Mary is separated. She has one year at her current residence. She has three years on the job with her current employer. She is 31.

Decision: Risk Category Rating: "B + "

Comments:

1. Being separated is a giant negative. The separation stage of a divorce is so traumatic and disruptive that an "A" rating cannot be given.

2. However, the fact that Mary has lived at her current residence for one year and has been working at the same job three years indicates that she is relatively stable and the separation activity has not yet significantly disrupted her lifestyle. Therefore, the "B + " credit rating is appropriate.

Analysis of Fig. 4–8. Bill has two years at his current address. The remainder of his form is not completely filled out.

Decision: Risk Category Rating: None

Patient Information

A B C

Date 11-1-87

Patient's Name: Crocker (Last) Thomas (First) P. (Middle)

Address: 12334 Fifth Street, Apt. 610 (Street) Monument (City) CO (State) 80100 (Zip)

Home Phone 555-1234 Birthdate 1-3-64 Social Security # 569-00-6856

If patient is a minor, give parent's or guardian's name n/a

Whom may we thank for referring you to our office? Yellow Pages

Responsible Party Information

Name: Same (Last) (First) (Middle) M (Marital Status)

Residence: Same (Street) (City) (State) (Zip)

Mailing Address: Same (Street) (City) (State) (Zip)

How long at this address 1 year Home Phone 555-1234 Work Phone 555-6778

Previous Address (if less than 3 yrs.): Hickam Air Force Base, Honolulu, HI 96700 (Street, City, State, Zip)

Social Security # See above Birthdate See above Relationship to Patient self

Employer U. S. Air Force Occupation Pilot - Captain No. Years Employed 3

Spouse's Name: Crocker (Last) Kelly (First) -- (Middle) Relationship to Patient wife

Employer Homemaker Occupation n/a No. Years Employed

Social Security # 568-00-4422 Birthdate 10-3-64 Work Phone ---

Insurance Information

Insured's Name ______ Insured's Soc. Sec. # ______

Insurance Company ______ Group No. ______ Local No. ______

Insurance Co. Address ______

Do you have dual coverage? Yes ☐ No ☐ If yes:

Insured's Name ______ Insured's Soc. Sec. # ______

Insurance Co. ______ Group No. ______ Local No. ______

Insurance Co. Address ______

Insured's Employer ______

Emergency Information

Name of nearest relative not living with you John A. Cross

Complete Address 1490 N. W. First St., Portland, OR 97229

Phone (503) 555-2421

I understand that where appropriate, credit bureau reports may be obtained.

Signature (Parent's signature if minor) Thomas P. Crocker

Updates (date & initial) ______ ______ ______ ______ ______

CONFIDENTIAL (for record and pretreatment evaluation)
Zuelke & Associates 1986

Fig. 4–6

Patient Information

A B C

Date 11-1-87

Patient's Name Wilson (Last) Dennis (First) T. (Middle)

Address 13005 N. W. Fir (Street) Portland (City) OR (State) 97222 (Zip)

Home Phone 555-5421 Birthdate 10-1-74 Social Security # ---

If patient is a minor, give parent's or guardian's name Mary R. Wilson

Whom may we thank for referring you to our office? Dr. Roth

Responsible Party Information

Name Wilson (Last) Mary (First) R. (Middle) Sep (Marital Status)

Residence 13005 N. W. Fir (Street) Portland (City) OR (State) 97222 (Zip)

Mailing Address same (Street) ____ (City) ____ (State) ____ (Zip)

How long at this address 1 year Home Phone see above Work Phone 555-6929

Previous Address (if less than 3 yrs.) 1400 N. W. Pine St., (Street) Portland, (City) OR (State) 97212 (Zip)

Social Security # 569-99-6000 Birthdate 11-1-57 Relationship to Patient mother

Employer Evans & Walker Occupation legal secretary No. Years Employed 3

Spouse's Name --- (Last) ____ (First) ____ (Middle) Relationship to Patient ____

Employer --- Occupation ____ No. Years Employed ____

Social Security # ____ Birthdate ____ Work Phone ____

Insurance Information

Insured's Name ____ Insured's Soc. Sec. # ____

Insurance Company ____ Group No. ____ Local No. ____

Insurance Co. Address ____

Do you have dual coverage? Yes ☐ No ☐ If yes:

Insured's Name ____ Insured's Soc. Sec. # ____

Insurance Co. ____ Group No. ____ Local No. ____

Insurance Co. Address ____

Insured's Employer ____

Emergency Information

Name of nearest relative not living with you Terry Harmon

Complete Address 1396 S. W. Devonburg Dr., Beaverton, OR 97000

Phone 555-2047

I understand that where appropriate, credit bureau reports may be obtained.

Signature (Parent's signature if minor) Mary Wilson

Updates (date & initial) ____ ____ ____ ____ ____

CONFIDENTIAL (for record and pretreatment evaluation)

Fig. 4–7

Patient Information

A B C

Date 9-15-87

Patient's Name Wirt (Last) Geneva (First) ______ (Middle)

Address Route 1, Box 502 (Street) Longview (City) WA (State) 83502 (Zip)

Home Phone 555-5094 Birthdate 1-9-59 Social Security # ______

If patient is a minor, give parent's or guardian's name ______

Whom may we thank for referring you to our office? ______

Responsible Party Information

Name Wirt (Last) Bill (First) ______ (Middle) ______ (Marital Status)

Residence same (Street) ______ (City) ______ (State) ______ (Zip)

Mailing Address same (Street) ______ (City) ______ (State) ______ (Zip)

How long at this address 2 years Home Phone 555-5094 Work Phone ______

Previous Address (if less than 3 yrs.) ______ (Street) ______ (City) ______ (State) ______ (Zip)

Social Security # ______ Birthdate ______ Relationship to Patient husband

Employer ______ Occupation ______ No. Years Employed ______

Spouse's Name ______ (Last) ______ (First) ______ (Middle) Relationship to Patient ______

Employer ______ Occupation ______ No. Years Employed ______

Social Security # ______ Birthdate ______ Work Phone ______

Insurance Information

Insured's Name Geneva Wirt Insured's Soc. Sec. # ______

Insurance Company Blue Cross Group No. ______ Local No. ______

Insurance Co. Address ______

Do you have dual coverage? Yes ☐ No ☐ If yes:

Insured's Name ______ Insured's Soc. Sec. # ______

Insurance Co. ______ Group No. ______ Local No. ______

Insurance Co. Address ______

Insured's Employer ______

Emergency Information

Name of nearest relative not living with you Bob Waters

Complete Address Miami, Florida

Phone ______

I understand that where appropriate, credit bureau reports may be obtained.

Signature (Parent's signature if minor) Geneva Wirt

Updates (date & initial) ______ ______ ______ ______ ______

CONFIDENTIAL (for record and pretreatment evaluation)
Zuelke & Associates 1986

Fig. 4–8

Comments:

1. You may have fallen into a trap here and given Mr. Wirt a "B" or "C" rating. This is normal because of the tendency to be conservative when granting credit. However, remember that the job of the financial secretary is to look for a reasonable way to grant credit to your prospective patients.

2. For instance, what if Mr. Wirt had 20 years on the job? And what if he had lived 15 years at his previous address in the same city? Knowing those facts would change your rating dramatically. But the fact is you don't have that information. Therefore, Mr. Wirt cannot be given a rating.

3. Also, keep in mind the damage that could be done to your practice if, on the basis of incomplete information, you rate a "C" patient an "A", or an "A" patient a "C." In the first case, you might not be able to collect for some services rendered or you would have a hard time collecting. This would not add to the well-being of your practice.

However, the second situation could cost your practice a great deal more. For instance, if you rated an "A" patient a "C" you would use aggressive and restrictive credit policies with that person. This may cause him to not accept your diagnosis, to reject your treatment, and to not refer friends and family. This could ultimately cost you thousands of dollars in lost production and revenue.

These are not arguments for rating a person higher than he should be. They are simply arguments for not rating a person on the basis of incomplete information.

From the seven examples that I have just discussed, you have seen that the ABC decision is subjective to a degree. Two people evaluating the same information may very well give the same patient different credit ratings. This will not be a problem as long as the people making the credit ratings 1) are doing so based on appropriate criteria as we have discussed, 2) do not have an emotional attachment to the patient, and 3) are able to take a pragmatic look at the situation and make the credit decision they believe is the most appropriate for the practice.

With this approach, along with a thorough understanding of the basic rules discussed so far in this chapter, the variations between credit ratings from any two or three persons would be very minor. From time to time, perhaps, there may be some disagreement on whether a patient is an "A+" or an "A" or whether a patient is an "A–" or a "B+." These differences are minor and will cause no serious negative impact on the practice. If, however, you are unable to determine if a patient is an "A" or a "B," a more serious review of your criteria should be made. There is such a significant difference between an "A" and "B" patient that indecision in this area could cause serious, negative repercussions for your practice.

Remember that your primary goal is to do everything possible to enable the patient to accept the diagnosed care. So, if you are ever in doubt whether a patient's credit rating is a "B+" or "A–," rate the patient an "A–." Where true doubt exists, give the patient the benefit of the doubt. In most cases, you will have little doubt as to the patient's credit rating.

I want to re-emphasize that we have made these credit decisions based solely on an evaluation of the information contained in a patient history form. In making this credit decision, we have not yet considered the credit bureau report or a past payment record. We have not considered any extraneous information that we may have learned about the patient. We have not taken into account any of our personal biases that may be present regarding race, marital status, financial status, or employment status. Rather, we have taken a pragmatic, practical look from the point of view of a loan officer. We have made our credit decision based on how this patient has chosen to live his life.

Additional information is often available that will assist in making an even more accurate credit decision on patients. These tools are used to supplement the credit decision that has already been made. These tools are: 1) a credit bureau report, and 2) a thorough review of the past payment record. Both of these will be discussed in the following chapter.

CHAPTER 5

SUPPLEMENTARY CREDIT EVALUATION TOOLS

Credit Bureau Report

In the previous chapter, I presented the primary means of qualifying your patients (that is, identifying the level of credit risk or potential credit risk): to evaluate thoroughly a completed and well-designed patient history form. It is also appropriate that you supplement that analysis with whatever additional information is available.

Additional information concerning your responsible party can be obtained from your credit bureau. The modern American credit bureau is a wonder. Today, in less than 60 seconds, a properly equipped dental office can obtain a detailed, point-by-point credit bureau report on virtually any adult human being in the United States. The credit bureau report will contain your patient's address, age and birthdate, Social Security number, previous addresses, employer, and probably previous employers for the last 10 years or so. This same information can be obtained on your patient's spouse.

The Modern American Credit Bureau

The story of today's credit bureau is very much the same as the story of the mom-and-pop grocery store. Many years ago, just like the mom-and-pop grocery store, credit bureaus were very, very small and there were many hundreds, if not thousands, of credit bureaus located in virtually all major cities and even most middle-sized cities in this country. The credit bureaus of the past maintained credit files that had been laboriously obtained by personal interviews, telephone calls, and extensive research of county court records. All of the information was collated under names and filed as handwritten documentation in voluminous filing cabinets. A creditor who had subscribed or become a member of the credit bureau would contact that bureau when he had need of obtaining credit information on a particular credit applicant. A credit bureau representative would then communicate to the credit grantor all of the information on file. If that information was current enough and sufficient for the creditor to make a credit decision, no further information was requested. However, if the credit bureau's information was skimpy or perhaps nonexistent, the creditor would request that the credit bureau update its files. The creditor would give the credit bureau any information that he or she had indicating the debts and creditors of the applicant. The credit bureau would then, personally and by phone, investigate each credit reference listed by the creditor and report back to the creditor their findings. A credit decision was very often based upon that additional information.

As with virtually all other information gathering, this method has been eliminated. Today almost all major creditors — Sears, GMAC, Ford Motor Credit, Wards, J. C. Penney, Macy's, Chevron Oil, American Express, VISA, MasterCard — are linked by computer to all the credit bureaus in this country. Every time you make a payment on a debt and every time you miss a payment on a debt, that information is reported monthly and in a few cases quarterly to every credit bureau in the nation. The information contained in the credit bureau's database is accurate to a high degree, primarily because of federal laws such as the Fair Credit Reporting Act. Also, additional information is made available to the credit bureaus by various federal, state, and county court systems. Every time a lawsuit is filed, every time a divorce or lien is filed, every time a judgment is entered, and every time a collection agency starts activity, that information becomes a part of public record which is reported and made a part of the affected party's personal credit bureau report.

Credit reports are extremely detailed. A report commonly includes:

1. Account numbers of the applicant's credit cards.
2. Date a particular account at a particular institution was opened.
3. Largest amount of money that was ever borrowed at that institution or the largest amount of money that was ever owed at that institution.
4. Credit limit on any individual credit card.
5. Current account balance.
6. Detailed record of that applicant's paying habits; also the number of times the account has been 30, 60, or 90 days past due is noted along with detailed information concerning any delinquency that was more serious, including lawsuits, bad debts, write-offs, and repossessions.

Over time and with the advent of computerization, a credit bureau centrally located in a major city could track not only the persons living in that city but also the persons living in all of the surrounding communities. And like many other industries, one credit bureau bought out the next, which bought out the next. Today, instead of thousands of credit bureaus in all of the towns throughout the country, there remain only five major ones. They are: Credit Bureau, Inc., in Atlanta, Georgia; Trans Union in Chicago, Illinois; ACS in Houston, Texas; Chilton in Dallas, Texas; and TRW in Orange, California.

These five credit bureaus maintain 99% of all of the credit information that is available on citizens in the United States today. Credit Bureau, Inc., out of Atlanta also maintains files on virtually the entire population of Canada.

Obtaining a Credit Report

At one time the only effective way of obtaining a credit report was to make contact with the credit bureau, request the information, and wait days, even weeks, to obtain a written report on the applicant. Written credit reports can still be obtained today from the credit bureaus upon request. These reports typically take from two to five days to arrive in the office and are quite expensive. (I do not recommend that this method be used to obtain credit reports.)

A second method of obtaining a report is to request the information by telephone. Using this technique, an office employee contacts a credit bureau operator, and gives the operator the patient's name, address, Social Security number, date of birth, etc. The operator enters that information into the computer, calling up the applicant's credit report on the video display terminal. The credit bureau operator reads the information the operator feels the office needs to make the credit decision. The office employee may write down the information. The end result will be 8 to 12 minutes spent on the phone, an approximate cost of $3.00 to $5.00 in credit bureau access fees, and a credit report that may or may not accurately reflect the applicant's actual credit history.

A third, more satisfying, less expensive, and more commonly used method of obtaining a credit report is to rent or purchase a small electronic device known as a data terminal. The typical data terminal is small enough that two devices can fit inside a standard-size briefcase. They are merely communication devices designed to communicate with a computer. In physical appearance they look much like a miniature typewriter.

Utilizing a data terminal, an office employee has only to dial a special credit bureau phone number, type in a 10–15 digit security code, and enter the patient's full name and address. Within 5 to 10 seconds, the data terminal will begin printing a hard copy of a completely detailed and very accurate credit report on your patient or responsible party. The cost of obtaining a report like this is one-half to one-third the cost of obtaining reports in any other manner. Obtaining reports by data terminal is the most effective way of learning about your patients' credit background.

At this point I want to address the need, or, more appropriately, the lack of need, to get your patient's permission to obtain a credit bureau report. Figure 5–1 is a duplicate of federal regulations governing credit bureaus and the usage of their reports. As you can see, a credit bureau report may be obtained for any permissible business use. In my opinion, it is not necessary to obtain specific permission from a credit applicant to obtain a credit report. However, I strongly recommend that you check with your own credit bureau and perhaps your own attorney before making any decisions in this regard. As you can see from the patient history forms in the previous chapter, I recommend that you include on your patient history form a statement as follows: "I understand that, where appropriate, credit bureau reports may be obtained." This statement is not intended to fulfill any legal obligation. However, in my experience, a statement such as this has not caused any problems with patients throughout the country and should actually avoid any potential problems with patients.

"§ 604. Permissible purposes of reports

"A consumer reporting agency may furnish a consumer report under the following circumstances and no other:

"(1) In response to the order of a court having jurisdiction to issue such an order.

"(2) In accordance with the written instructions of the consumer to whom it relates.

"(3) To a person which it has reason to believe—

"(A) intends to use the information in connection with a credit transaction involving the consumer on whom the information is to be furnished and involving the extension of credit to, or review or collection of an account of, the consumer; or

"(B) intends to use the information for employment purposes; or

"(C) intends to use the information in connection with the underwriting of insurance involving the consumer; or

"(D) intends to use the information in connection with a determination of the consumer's eligiblity for a license or other benefit granted by a governmental instrumentality required by law to consider an applicant's financial responsibility or status; or

"(E) otherwise has a legitimate business need for the information in connection with a business transaction involving the consumer.

Fig. 5–1

How to Use a Credit Report

Once you become familiar with the format or layout of a credit report, you will quickly see that these reports contain a tremendous amount of information, much of which is not necessarily useful to you. There is information regarding credit limits, account balances, minimum monthly payments that are due, dates and sources of other inquiries of this particular person's credit bureau report, and so on. Much of this information is useful to a loan officer who needs to determine his applicant's debt ratio and, perhaps, is interested in discovering hidden debts. In a health care office, however, you have already made your basic credit decision when you reviewed the patient history form. Therefore, a credit report should be used solely to determine whether or not your responsible party pays his bills and how well he pays them. Is he always current? Is he usually current? Is he 60 and 90 days past due frequently? Has he been written off as uncollectible, filed bankruptcy, or had repossessions?

A financial secretary reviewing a credit report will take no more than 30 seconds to review the report as a check on her credit decision. Again, the basic credit decision is made when the patient history form is reviewed. Reviewing the credit bureau report is a backup, a safeguard.

Using Credit Reports: An Example

Clearly, in my first example of the patient history forms, Tom Simmons was an "A+" patient. What if a credit report was reviewed which indicated that Tom had never paid a bill in his life, had been written off as uncollectible, had had his cars and kitchen appliances repossessed by various creditors, and had been written off as uncollectible by other health care providers in the community? Certainly a situation such as this will come up from time to time. The "A+" rating in a case such as this will be replaced with a "C" rating and the patient, financially speaking, will be handled appropriately.

A thoroughly reviewed credit report is a wonderful tool to support your credit decisions and to help you avoid making serious mistakes in your credit evaluations. Its primary use is to give you some assurance that your "A+" rating was, indeed, accurate. Sometimes it is scary to be qualifying a patient as an "A+," which means he may obtain almost unlimited credit from your office. Reviewing a credit report which shows that this patient has never missed a payment to any of his creditors in the past 20 years should make your decision to grant liberal credit much more comfortable.

Why Use a Data Terminal

The average credit report obtained via a data terminal costs $2.00, although I have recently seen them as inexpensive as $.95 and as expensive as $2.50. When purchased, data terminals cost anywhere from $300 at some electronic stores to $1,000 from certain credit bureaus. They can also be rented from most credit bureaus throughout the country for a fee of $15 to $40 per month.

Very little training is needed to learn to utilize a data terminal and to read and evaluate a credit bureau report. In all areas of the country the local credit bureau will provide information and training in the use of data terminals and the evaluation of the credit bureau report, free of charge. They will not, of course, understand the ABC rating I have talked about and will not be able to assist you in relating a credit bureau report to a credit evaluation.

Despite the ease of use and low costs associated with data terminals, I continue to come across practices that are resistant to using this technology. The reasons for the resistance are varied, and I would like to address a few of them.

For some, the cost of renting or purchasing a data terminal and the cost of maintaining membership in a credit bureau and obtaining credit reports is one more bit of overhead expense when overhead is already too high. If you were a member of the most expensive credit bureau in the entire United States and if you obtained credit reports on 40 patients a month, your total overhead, including rental of a data terminal and the cost of the reports, would be less than $1,800 a year. I ask you, how much is peace of mind worth? Wouldn't it be worth $1,800 a year to know that you are not granting credit to patients who are unable or unwilling to pay you? Or conversely, that you are granting credit to someone who has always paid all of his bills and has never had a delinquency problem? In most cases the total cost associated with credit bureau membership and usage is far lower.

A quick review of the delinquency that is currently present in your office (much of which would have been avoided had you obtained a credit report prior to starting care) should convince you that becoming a member of a credit bureau and using it on a regular basis will be one of the most cost-effective things you have ever done for your practice.

What's in a Credit Report

The next two figures will show two different credit reports from two different credit bureaus. They are not presented to teach you how to read a report, but rather to give you a basic understanding of what a credit report looks like, to show you the different formats the different credit bureaus have, and to show you how a credit decision can be made from the information contained in a credit report.

Figure 5–2 is a report from the Trans Union credit bureau in Chicago. It includes the date and time the report was obtained. The following is an explanation of the items on the report by item number:

1. Date this person's file was originally generated with the credit bureau.

2. Responsible party's full name as it has been recorded by the credit bureau.

3. Social Security number.

4. Last known current address.

5. Employer.

6. Birth month and year of the responsible party.

7. Address reported immediately prior to the current address.

8. Date that address (Item 7) became available to the credit bureau.

9. Prior address recorded.

10. Headings to identify the information listed below.

11. Name of the creditor.

12. Creditor's credit bureau membership number.

13. Date the responsible party's account opened with creditor.

14. HICR - Highest amount ever owed creditor or the credit limit.

15. DTRP/TERM - Date this information was reported to the credit bureau.

16. Balance as of that date.

17. MAX DEL - Maximum amount the account has ever been delinquent.

```
 I SMITH,JAMES,D,,MARY* 1470 NORTHWEST 124,PORTLAND,OR,97200*5  000-00-0000*
                                    ①
 TRANS UNION CREDIT REPORT   DATE: 03/17/88  TIME:  16:20
                                          2/82
②SMITH, JAMES D                             ③000-00-0000
④1470 NORTHWEST 123, PORTLAND, OR 97200            10 PT
⑤SMITH & SMITH                                   8/87R
    ⑥12/47
                                                                 555-0000
⑦1234 NW MAIN ST., PORTLAND, OR., 1000 97229      ⑧2/82R       7/87R
⑨10000C⑪POB 100000, PORTLAND OR. 97200                         2/82R
⑩SUB NAME/ACCT# ⑫SUB#  ⑬OPEND  ⑭HICR ⑮DTRP/TERM ⑯BAL/MAX. ⑰DEL ⑱PAY.PAT/HIST MOP

⑲DINERS CLUB     N5500     6/86 I $9730   12/87P      $0     $0   112111111111 001
 3800000000                                                         12  1  0  0

 AMERICAN EXPR   N600000 10/87 I  $120    1/88A    $272     $0   1               001
 3700000000000

⑳BEN FRANKLIN    B5010    12/87 I $19K    1/88A $19741     $0 0 11               I01
 8500000000        DCKW T     ESM00000J   ㉑M235                    1 0 0 0

㉒BNFICIAL-BNCHG F660000   8/87 I $495     1/88A   $289          11               I01
 41400000000000               UK         ㉓12M

㉔FARWEST PER CL B5000     8/84 C $50K     1/88A $24728     $0 0 1111             R01
 7800000000000000             UK$5000    MIN495                 12  0 0 0

 1ST INTERSTATE B65689   10/86 C $20K     1/88A $12214     $0 0 111111111111 C01
 5130000000000                           10M395                 15  0 0 0

 FST INTERSTATE B5000     3/86 C $15K   12/87C    $0       $0   1111111111     I01
 30000000000000

 SEARS ROEBUCK  D50       5/75 U $866   12/87P    $0       $0 0 111111X111X1 R01
 090000000                                X29                   24  0 0 0

㉕FIRST CARD     B26       7/87   $4900  10/87A $4799      $0 0 11               $01
 46000000                        $8000

 INQR   6  DATE    ECOA SUBCODE          SUBNAME           TYPE   AMT
          3/17/88    I  MC03003(DAY)     JOHN SMITH

 **END OF CREDIT REPORT**
 REPORT SERVICED BY:
 TRANS UNION CREDIT INFORMATION, NORTHWEST DIV.
```

Fig. 5–2

18. PAY.PAT/HIST - Responsible party's paying habits over the most recent 12 months. Most credit bureaus rate delinquency according to the following formula: 0 — too new to rate or account never used; 1 — account current/paid as agreed/$0 account balance; 2—30 days late; 3 — 60 days late; 4 — 90 days late; 5 — 120 days late or more; 7 — bankruptcy; 8 — repossession; 9 — uncollectible/bad debt/write off/etc. (#6 is not used.)

19. Indicates that Diners Club opened an account with this person in June 1986, and that this person has owed as much as $9,730. This information was received by the credit bureau in December 1987. This person's account balance at that time was $0. He had never been delinquent, and out of the last 12 months, 11 payments were made on time and one was 30 days late. (This is not a conflict with the $0 under the term Max. Del because many times creditors will report the delinquency in the column under payment history and will not utilize the column Max. Del)

20. Indicates that Benjamin Franklin made a loan to this person in December 1987 for approximately $19,000. In January 1988 the account balance was $19,741. There was no delinquency. They had only reviewed two payments, both of which were current.

21. Indicates that this person was making a monthly payment of $235.

22. Indicates that Beneficial opened an account for this person in August 1987 in the amount of $495. As of January 1988, the account balance was $289. For the benefit of the credit bureau, they had reviewed only the most recent two payments, both of which were current.

23. Indicates that this was a 12-month contract.

24. Indicates that this person has a personal line of credit with Farwest in the amount of $50,000 that was opened in August 1984. In January 1988, the balance of the credit line was $24,728. Of the most recent four payments reviewed, all were current. The minimum monthly payment for this person is $495.

25. Indicates that First Card (VISA) opened an account in July 1987 with a credit limit of $8,000. The highest amount this person has ever charged on this card was $4,900. As of October 1987, this balance was $4,799 and his account was current.

This person's credit is impeccable. Assuming that you identified him as an "A+" on a patient history form, the credit report would certainly support that decision.

Fig 5–3 is a report from Credit Bureau, Inc., of Atlanta, Georgia, as obtained through their subsidiary in Metairie, Louisiana.

1. This patient has been on file with this particular credit bureau since March of 1984.

2. The most recent address the credit bureau has, which was current as of February, 1988.

```
NM-NM

NM-LINE IS TOO LONG

NM-DOE,JOHN,Q.
CA-108,12T,ST,ANYTOWN,US,00000
ID-SSS-000-00-0000*5.

*  198 CBI
               (1)
* DOE,JOHN,Q.  SINCE 03/17/84   FAD 02/15/88         FN-008
(2) 1234,E MAIN,ST,ANYTOWN,US,00000,CRT RPTD 02/88
 5678,BROADWAY,ANYTOWN,US,00000,DAT RPTD 05/87
(3) BDS-08/30/54,SSS-000-00-0000
(4) 01 ES-,TEXACO ANYTOWN

  *SUM-03/80-01/88,PR/OI-YES,FB-NO, ACCTS:15,HC$0-11676, 4-ONES, 1-EIGHT,
     7-NINES, 3-OTHERS.

(5)***** PUBLIC RECORDS OR OTHER INFORMATION *****
(6)02 02/88 BKRPT 000ZZ00,88-00000,LIAB$37537,ASSET$34011,EXEMPT$800,
             INDIVID,PERSONAL,VOL
(7)03 01/87 W E P 000ZZ00, 8700000,LIAB$19470,ASSET$52510,INDIVID,PERSONAL
             C 13
(8)04 03/87*COLL 01/87 000YY000 FOR CLIENT UNKNOWN,$35,03/87 UNPAID
               BAL-03/87 $35,    DLA: 12/84, I,9400000
  05 03/87*COLL 01/87 000YY000 FOR CLIENT UNKNOWN,$49,03/87 UNPAID
               BAL-03/87 $49,    DLA: 06/85  I,9400001
(9)06 07/86 JUDG,000ZZ000, $11336,DEF-J WITH JANE DOE,17000,ST JAMES
               BANK AND TRUST,VER 08/86
   ********************************************

 *INQS-SHELL         905000000    06/27/87   CITLINE/SS 801000000 05/30/87
      1ST BKCARD   4900000000    01/07/87

    FIRM/ID CODE          RPTD  OPND  H/C TRM  BAL P/D CS  MR ECOA ACCOUNT NUM
(10)ASSOC FIN *490000000  01/88 08/86 1007 24M 1007     I9     J      9051-00000
  T-CHG/NCNB*900000       01/88 09/80 1146      598 598 R9     I        87000000
     30(00)60(01)90(01) 02/87-R5,01/87-R4,12/86-R3                    DLA 10/86
  ASSOC FIN *490000003  12/87 08/86    0          0     I9     J      5340-00000
     30(00)60(01)90(00) 10/85-I3                                      DLA-12/87
     ACCOUNT TRANSFERRED
(11)1ST FIN    *4950000   11/87 04/86 6289 203 6110 2K+ I8     I      5100000000
     30(   )60(   )90(  ) 05/87-I5,04/87-I5,03/87-I5                  DLA 10/86
  PHILLIPS  *9000000      09/87            0          0     O9     U      67-000-000
     PAID CHARGE OFF
  TEXACO USA*90500000    08/87 07/80 1151             0     R9     I      532000000
     PAID CHARGE OFF
  ANYTOWN      49500000   07/87 ACCOUNT INCLUDED IN BANKRUPTCY             A0000
     NO ACTIVITY SINCE DATE REPORTED
     ACCOUNT CHARGED TO PROFIT AND LOSS
  GECC       *90600000    04/87 ACCOUNT INCLUDED IN BANKRUPTCY    C000000-B10
  FNBC VISA *4950N00      03/87 ACCOUNT INCLUDED IN BANKRUPTCY        43100000
  ANBCRCARD *160000000   05/86 06/84 1075             0     R9     U  58200000000
     30(01)60(00)90(00) 03/85-R2                                      DLA 12/84
  BLAZER     *495F000000 04/86 10/84 3782 36M      0 I1   I7     I        1800000
  1ST FIN    *495FS00     10/84 03/84 1633 24M      0 I1   O6     I      118000000
  FORD MO CR 495FA00      12/84 03/84  11K             I9          I    A100000000
```

Fig. 5–3

3. Date of birth and Social Security number.

4. Employer.

5. Public record is highlighted and listed. Public record information is on file at the local county court house and is information which is a matter of public record. In many cases public record information is very seriously negative.

6. The patient filed bankruptcy in February, 1988.

7. In January, 1987, the patient filed a Chapter 13 bankruptcy.

8. A $35 account was written off as uncollectible and assigned to a collection agency.

9. The patient was sued for $11,336 by St. James Bank and Trust.

10. A local finance company reported in January, 1988, on a loan that opened in August, 1986. The patient had borrowed $1,007 and had promised to repay the loan in 24 months. The balance in January, 1988, was $1,007, and the account was written off as uncollectible.

11. An account was opened with another finance company in April of 1986 for a loan on merchandise which was later repossessed for non-payment (I8).

Clearly you do not need to go into the details of the rest of this credit report as this patient is certainly a weak "C" patient. Any practice not having a death wish would decline to grant credit to a patient such as this.

This would be a good time to recognize that this person's patient history form might have looked wonderful. He is married, he is in his 30's, he has a good job, and he has been in this area for a long time. Had you not been willing to use a credit bureau to obtain this information, you may have granted this patient extensive credit, resulting in serious financial loss and hardship for the practice.

Final Words on Credit Reports

In summary, the credit report can be a valuable asset to the financial secretary and to the health care practice. Although a credit report should be obtained on each new patient, it is not to be used as a crutch. The information obtained from reviewing a credit report should be used solely to support the credit decision already made, based on a thorough review of a properly completed patient history form.

Past Payment History

There is one other item that needs to be evaluated. It is an item that is unfortunately ignored by many health care office financial secretaries: How has the responsible party paid in the past? Many of the patients you are granting credit to have been or are currently patients of record in your office. Therefore, it is most appropriate that you pay special attention to how they have handled their account with you.

It is rare that I have ever been in an office where I was unable to identify a seriously delinquent patient—perhaps even a patient who was going to be written off as uncollectible—that had not been identified as a serious problem prior to the time the most recent work was performed. It is inconceivable to me that a practice would provide additional care of a nonemergency nature and grant additional credit to a patient under these circumstances.

As mentioned in a previous chapter, you need only to review your own delinquency and you will undoubtedly be able to uncover a number of cases where patients were delinquent on a previous balance when additional care was provided. You will certainly recall my earlier comments about the desire to remain comfortable and/or the reluctance to do anything that may cause discomfort. This reluctance to be uncomfortable is the primary cause for this type of delinquency.

Once you start to review credit reports, you will learn that once a person in our society has developed a history of being delinquent on his debts he will, most likely, continue those payment habits for the rest of his adult life. I am not saying that a person never changes or does not have temporary financial difficulty which he is later able to overcome. Certainly those situations do occur. I am only stating that they happen in the minority of cases.

The vast majority of times (90+%) the tiger will not change his stripes. Or should I say, the skunk will not change his stripes. Since neither you, nor I, nor the finest credit manager in the world has the ability to identify in advance which people with weak paying habits are going to rehabilitate themselves and become exemplary patients, it is absolutely necessary that we pay attention to the facts as they present themselves.

What the Facts Can Reveal

If you have a patient who has been rude, discourteous, or uncooperative in the past, the odds are tremendously high that he will continue to be that way in the future. If you have a patient who has made intermittent or sporadic payments, payments less than he had agreed to pay, or payments less than what is appropriate to the account balance, this behavior is likely to continue. If you have a patient who has not responded appropriately to past collection activity, the odds are tremendously high that this activity will continue as you provide additional care.

Dealing with this type of patient is more difficult, at least emotionally, than is dealing with a new patient. In many cases these delinquent accounts or uncooperative patients have been in the practice for years. With a new patient you may be perfectly willing to demand cash only or demand a major down payment and limit the financial arrangements to a very few months. However, when faced with a patient you have known for years, or who has been in the practice for a long time, quite often the doctor, the financial secretary, and even the entire staff can get cold feet. Unfortunately, there is no easy solution to this problem.

Clearly, if your primary interest is in the overall well-being of the practice, if you are truly committed to eliminating the types of problems addressed in this book, then you need to handle these patients appropriately—whether they have been in the practice for 10 days or 10 years. If handling a patient "appropriately" causes that patient to become upset or, in the extreme, to leave the practice, then that would be an acceptable if unfortunate result. My assertion is that this kind of patient is not contributing to the well-being of the practice. In fact, he or she is actively damaging the well-being of the practice. Therefore, unless you are able to bring this kind of patient under absolute, total control, he does not deserve to be in your practice.

This is an appropriate time to bring up an alternative which was discussed earlier. When faced with providing additional care to patients with a history of inappropriate financial behavior concerning their accounts, and who are unable to pay in an appropriate manner for new care (or if you are unwilling to deal appropriately with them because of their past relationship with the practice), then the work should be performed at no charge. This recommendation is not made lightly. In fact, it is made in absolute seriousness. How could a health care practitioner in good faith hold his financial secretary accountable to maintain receivables at appropriate levels, to maintain delinquency at appropriate levels, and to maintain his monthly cash flow at appropriate levels, if he is going to force her to continue to deal with known problem patients?

Another Factor to Consider

In reviewing a patient's past history and in making your decision about how that patient should be handled in the future, another item needs to be considered. I mention this item at some risk of creating confusion.

In most health care practices the vast majority of delinquent accounts—even seriously delinquent accounts—are patients with impeccable levels of integrity throughout the community, patients with perfect credit who would never dream of missing a payment to Sears or Wards, on their car or their house, or on any other financial obligation. Why is this the case? Because their doctor has been training them for years that it is perfectly acceptable to pay the doctor in an inappropriate manner. The old adage that "the doctor always gets paid last" is, in my experience, very true. But it is true only because the doctor asks last.

If when reviewing a patient's past payment record, you find the past payment record unsatisfactory, it is necessary you consider how your practice has handled that patient's delinquency in the past. Have you trained that patient with your lack of collection activity to believe it is acceptable to be delinquent? When a patient sends you a payment which is less than he agreed to send you, did you post the payment and fail to communicate with the patient? I am suggesting that much of your existing delinquency has been created by your own activity or, perhaps, lack of activity. When reviewing a patient's past payment record, take your role into consideration. However, do not assume that every patient who is delinquent in the office is delinquent simply because you did not have good collection policies in the practice.

CHAPTER 6

PRESENTING THE OFFICE POLICY

By now, you should have an excellent understanding of my philosophy. To build quality of life within the practice, you must nurture and support your quality patients (the patients who will contribute to your well-being), and you must control and, where necessary, eliminate those patients who will not or cannot contribute to your well-being. This philosophy is demonstrated by granting liberal credit to those patients who qualify for it, and granting little or no credit to those who don't.

It is one thing to *have* such a policy in your practice. But a policy such as this is of no value unless your patients are aware that the policy exists. This point is even more important for those offices that are contemplating switching or changing policies in "mid-stream," so to speak.

If your practice has historically been fairly aggressive in handling credit (you have subscribed to the "payment-at-time-of-service" philosophy) and you are planning to change that philosophy to something along the lines of what you are reading in this book, it is going to be important that you educate your patients. You must educate your *new* patients. But even more important, you must educate *existing* patients. You must tell them that you have a new policy and that this policy is significantly different from the one you have had in the past.

One of the first things I do when I arrive in a new client's office is walk through the front door and take a good look at the reception area. I look for indications that the practice has an aggressive policy; specifically, office brochures and signs on the walls or on the front counter saying, "Payment is appreciated at the time services are rendered," or worse, "Payment is expected at the time services are rendered."

Office Policy: The Patient's Perception

Let's see what might happen in a practice that has a sign out front such as I just described. Unknown to the patient, if the practice is pressed, it will grant a patient credit, but only if the patient specifically asks for credit.

In this situation it is realistic to assume that a patient could come into the practice for a prophy, exam and x-rays, pay for that treatment, and leave. As far as the doctor is concerned, everything went smoothly. He had a nice new patient in the practice, and he could look forward to a long and satisfying relationship with that patient. However, that patient did not schedule the crown prep that had been diagnosed. Six months later that patient comes back for the recall, pays for the prophy and exam again and leaves. The doctor diagnoses that same tooth as needing a crown, and again the patient does not schedule. This is an excellent example of the type of patient who falls through the cracks in a dental office. This happens not because of the office's financial policy, but because of the patient's perception of what the policy is. Remember that this patient's only formal training concerning the office's financial policy was the sign on the front counter. This patient, having no information to the contrary, may very well believe that the office "requirement" is that she pay for that crown at the time services are rendered as well. She certainly needs the crown — she may even want the crown — but she does not want it badly enough to pay for it all at once. Because many patients are not likely to specifically request credit, they will very often avoid the issue altogether and never schedule to have such work done.

An even more graphic example of this type of damage is when the practice has a no-show/cancellation rate in hygiene of more than 3% to 5%. If you have more than three to five no-shows or cancels out of every 100 hygiene patients, you should look closely at your existing financial policy, or at your patients' perception of what your financial policy is. If you have required payment at the time of service in the past (especially for inexpensive treatments such as prophies and exams), or if the patient believes this is your policy, in my experience you can count on a higher-than-acceptable no-show rate in your hygiene department. It is not that your patients do not want their teeth cleaned, and it is certainly not that your patients are mad, angry, or upset with you or your practice. But very often the fee for a prophy and exam may not be comfortable for them to pay at that particular time. It is far easier to come up with a wonderful reason why they need to postpone and reschedule than to confess they are short of cash and to ask if they can pay in a few weeks. Without a solution to this problem, you will quickly and easily lose patients from your practice.

A Solution to Patient Misperception

Obviously the solution is to have a method of educating your new patients and re-educating your existing patients about your office financial policy. There are a number of ways to accomplish this. Probably the most successful method is to develop an office administrative brochure. I call it an "administrative" brochure because the purpose of the brochure is to educate the patients on the administrative policies of the practice. I have seen many practices that have developed an office brochure but have used it as their marketing or PR brochure as well as using it to present office hours and administrative policies. It is filled with material including photographs of the staff and the doctor, educational background information on the doctor, personal family history of the doctor, and even the clinical details of the areas of dentistry the doctor is primarily interested in.

However, the purpose of the brochure is to educate patients as quickly and as efficiently as possible, and a brochure will only do the job if it is clean and simple. It is not realistic to give a patient a two-to-six-page document and expect him to read through it carefully. This type of brochure is more often a tribute to the doctor's ego rather than a practical tool for the office. If it is necessary to present personal, clinical, or other marketing information to your patients or your prospective patients, then a separate brochure presenting that material should be developed.

Presentation of the Brochure

The design of an administrative brochure is important but only in order to appropriately display the information you want to communicate. But no matter how well designed a brochure is, no matter how much money, time, and effort have gone into the development and printing of the brochure, it will be useless unless it is read by your patients.

I frequently go into a dental office and see a brochure presentation rack in the reception area. Invariably these racks hold anywhere from one to ten different brochures — some of which are administrative in nature, some of which are clinical, and some of which are marketing or PR related. But when I interview the staff, I find they rarely, if ever, have to replenish the brochures in the rack. The comment I hear most often is, "Oh, they never read those." Yet, at least in the case of the administrative brochure, this is information that may be critical to your patients.

The only method that I have ever discovered that is universally effective in educating the patients is to physically and individually present the brochure to each new patient. By presenting the brochure I do not mean it is attached on a clipboard along with a patient history form. By presentation I mean that it is physically handed to a patient with a comment such as, "Mrs. Smith, this is our office brochure which explains some of our policies and procedures. It is important to us that you take the time to read it. Please let us know if you have any questions."

I recognize that a presentation such as this takes time, and in a busy dental office time is at a premium. But remember this one presentation may make the difference whether or not that patient accepts the diagnosis you make in the operatory.

When faced with making substantial changes in administrative policy, most of our clients have developed this brochure and, in addition to presenting it to all new patients, have chosen to mail it one time to all active patients of record. If you are going to change your policies, your patients have a right to be so informed. Since these changes are going to enable your patients to accept more of your diagnosis and care, it is in your best interest that they be informed of your new policies as quickly as possible.

Contents of the Administrative Brochure

Again, the policies presented in this brochure should be those that will affect the patient's business relationship with your practice. Will you offer financial arrangements? Do you accept assignment of insurance benefits? Will you handle insurance-related problems on your patient's behalf? Will you complete and file your patient's insurance? Do you offer a discount for payment at the time of treatment? Do you require down payments on your financial arrangements? Do you charge interest? At what rate? Is interest charged only on late payments? Or on account balances that are late? Or on accounts that are aged over a certain period of time? Do you have late charges? If so, when are they assessed and how much are they? Do you send statements? What are your office hours? How do you handle emergencies?

The office policy I recommend for our clients is to present policies in a section of the brochure that is central and likely to draw the patient's eye, as shown below.

Fee and Payment Policy. In an effort to keep dental costs down while maintaining a high level of professional care, we have established the following as our financial policy. Our fees may be paid as follows:

1. *Prepayment or payment at the time of treatment with a 5% discount (10% for orthodontics).* Prepayment saves us time and the expense of billing, enabling us to provide this valuable service. If you have dental insurance, we will offer this discount for payment of your portion of the fee that is not covered by insurance.

2. *Payment of the balance in full within 10 days of statement date.*

3. *Use of your VISA, MasterCard, or American Express.* Extended payments are available upon special request. All account balances outstanding more than 60 days from treatment date will bear interest at 1 1/2% per month or 18% per year. All major treatment and any treatment involving a laboratory procedure will require an appropriate down payment. Our senior citizens aged 62 and over will receive a 10% discount for payment at the time of treatment.

Insurance. If you have dental insurance, we will help you determine the coverage you have available. We ask that you assign your insurance benefits to this office. The balance will be arranged for you to pay as listed above. Professional care is provided to you, our patient, and not to an insurance company. Thus, the insurance company is ultimately responsible to the patient, and the patient is responsible to the doctor. We will help in every way we can, however, in filing your insurance claim and handling insurance questions from our office on your behalf.

Summary

This financial policy is designed with the general dentist in mind, but is also appropriate for all specialists other than orthodontists. Doctors with specialties which generate fairly high average fees such as periodontists, prosthodontists, endodontists, and oral surgeons may choose to charge interest after 90 days instead of 60 days. An orthodontist would probably offer a 10% discount for payment at the time treatment is started, rather than a 5% discount. And an orthodontist would not charge interest on his open accounts. Also, some doctors may not find the senior citizen discount appropriate, especially doctors in retirement communities.

Whether this brochure is inexpensive or quite costly, whether it is well designed or poorly designed, whether it is stilted or masterful prose, remember that it is useless unless it is read by your patients and read prior to the time that treatment is diagnosed and presented to the patient. Remember to re-educate your existing patients when you change your office policies. They have a right to know, and you want them to know, because the new policy may make it easier for them to accept your future diagnoses.

Many financial secretaries have had their job of conducting financial arrangements made easier because of the patient's understanding of the financial policy before the treatment plan was presented to him. Use your administrative brochure wisely. You will make your financial secretary's job easier and increase the overall well-being of your practice.

CHAPTER 7

OFFERING DISCOUNTS

There is some controversy regarding whether or not it is appropriate to offer discounts for payment at the time of treatment. My position is simply this: offering discounts works extremely well when used in conjunction with the other types of policies and procedures that I recommend.

Why Offer Discounts?

You will recall that I recommend offering your quality patients — the "A" patients — whatever reasonable financial arrangements they might need in order to encourage them to accept the diagnosis. I have already discussed the value to the growth of the practice of offering deserving patients financial arrangements on treatment plans. I am also aware, however, of the damage that would be done to the practice if every eligible patient (which we have agreed is the vast majority of all patients) chose to pay over a period of time, even if each patient made a substantial down payment and made financial arrangements over a limited period of time. It is necessary, therefore, to offer your patients inducements not to take advantage of the generous terms you are willing to offer. A discount for payment at the time of treatment is perhaps the most effective inducement you can offer.

How to Offer the Inducement

As stated in the financial policies of the office brochure, my recommendation is that a practice offer a 5% discount for payment at the time of treatment. By "at the time of treatment" I mean *on* or *before* the date treatment is started. I do not recommend that a discount be offered for payment by the time treatment is completed or for any financial arrangement other than payment on or before the date treatment is actually *started*.

Many clients ask, "If 5% works well, wouldn't a 10% discount work better? If so, why not offer a 10% discount?" It is true that if offering a 5% discount encourages a certain percentage of patients to pay at the time treatment is rendered, then offering a 10% discount would be even more effective. However, it is the obligation of the practitioner to utilize policies in his office that are fiscally appropriate. After years of evaluating this policy, it has become clear that when effectively presented, a 5% discount works to encourage patients to pay at the time treatment is rendered. Although a 10% discount would work better, it is my opinion that the increased number of patients who would pay in full as a result of the 10% discount is not sufficient to make up for the loss of profit due to the additional 5% discount.

How Not to Offer the Inducement

I have seen many offices with a 5% discount policy in effect, but it is offered only for payment of charges above a certain dollar amount; for instance, on charges of $100 or more. In determining whether or not this policy is appropriate, you should consider again the basis for offering the discount in the first place — to encourage your patients to pay at the time treatment is rendered. If the discount is not offered on charges under $100 and if you do not charge interest, then it is in your patient's best interest to wait and pay you as soon as they get the bill (in 30 days or so) or, worse, to make a payment or two on those charges. Since there is no incentive such as a cash discount for paying a $90 fee at the time treatment is rendered, the option of waiting may seem attractive to many of your patients. To overcome this problem, many doctors have made it "policy" to require payment at the time of treatment for fees totaling less than $100. With this policy, your patients are paying you because they *have to* because it is "your policy." They are not paying you because they *choose to*.

Summary

If you are going to run an effective business office in a health care practice, you need to get as much money as possible paid at the time of treatment. The damage to a practice of "requiring" payment at time of service is so substantial in lack of acceptance of care, no-shows, and last-minute cancellations, that I cannot support this policy. For this reason, I recommend a discount for payment of any and all charges, regardless of dollar amount, as long as those charges are paid *on or before* the day services are rendered.

A Special Case: Orthodontics. In spite of my previous comment regarding the difference between the 5% and 10% discounts, I recommend that orthodontists offer a 10% discount for cash, instead of 5%. This is not because the average orthodontic case fee is higher. Rather, it is because the alternative in an orthodontic office is for financial arrangements to be spread out over a long period of time. It is not reasonable for a general dentist to offer a 24-month financial arrangement on $3,000 worth of crown and bridge work. But it is reasonable to expect an orthodontist to offer 24 monthly payments on $3,000 worth of orthodontic care. This is primarily because treatment in the orthodontic office may very well take 24 months. In order to encourage patients to pay for orthodontics at the time of treatment, a larger discount needs to be offered. In my experience, a 10% discount does an excellent job.

Discounts and Insurance. As mentioned in the office policy brochure, if a patient has insurance for his general dental work or his orthodontic care, the insurance payment should be estimated, and the discount should be offered on the *patient's portion* of the fee not covered by insurance. I have seen many doctors offer a discount for payment of the entire case fee at the time treatment is rendered, even though these patients have dental insurance. This policy presents two problems, both of which are significant.

First, if a doctor has offered a discount to a patient and has been paid in full and then bills the insurance company for the full case fee, he has perpetrated insurance fraud. It is clear that a doctor may not sign an insurance form for a dental fee that is larger than he actually intends to collect from a patient. There have been more than a few cases of insurance companies prosecuting doctors who were practicing this policy.

Second, if a discount is offered to a patient with dental insurance for payment of his entire case fee and the discounted fee is reported to the insurance company, then although you will not have any problems with the insurance company, you may have problems with the patients. In many instances the patient has just been cut out of some of his insurance benefits.

For example, let's say your fee is $200 and the insurance is going to pay 80% of that or $160. If you offer your patient a discount for payment of that fee at the time of treatment and, therefore, discount the fee by $10, the patient would owe you $190. Then, if you bill insurance for $190, the insurance company will pay 80% or $152 instead of the $160 they would have paid in the first instance. You have cut your patient out of $8 of his/her benefit.

Because of the vast number of physicians, dentists, chiropractors, osteopaths, etc., who are offering discounts on the patient's portion of the fee not covered by insurance, I have taken the position that although this policy is generally unacceptable to insurance companies it is something they are willing to live with. I do not know of a single instance where a doctor has ever been prosecuted by an insurance company for practicing this policy.

I must caution you, however, that although my clients practice this policy, I am not an attorney and do not give legal advice. If you have concerns in this area, check with your own insurance companies and, perhaps, your own attorney before implementing a policy such as I have described.

CHAPTER 8

CHARGING INTEREST

As you saw from the office brochure presented earlier, I recommend all dental professionals, except orthodontists, charge interest after a certain time period on all balances. You are not in the lending business; therefore, the interest charge is used the same way that the discount is used: as an incentive for your patients not to choose long-term financial arrangements. In many cases, the 5% discount is not enough inducement to encourage patients to pay at the time of treatment. If the patient is presented with the option of paying over four to six months on an interest-free basis, that option may appear quite attractive. Any student of economics would understand that if a person could make monthly payments interest-free over any period of time, that is financially more attractive than turning loose of hard-earned capital all at once. How many of us, for instance, would not borrow money tomorrow or buy a nicer house or a nicer car if the financing were available on an interest-free basis? This is true with dentistry as well.

Charging Interest: Recommendations

My recommendation for most practices is that interest be charged on all outstanding balances after 60 days from date of treatment. This will allow your patients to pay you a few monthly payments — one-third down, 1/3 in 30 days, and 1/3 in 60 days, without any interest charge and will, of course, allow insurance the time to pay without any interest charges accumulating. I have tested this policy with 30, 60, and 90 days, and have found that 60 days works the best. It allows patients to make a few payments interest-free, it allows insurance to pay without interest accumulating, and it is viewed by your patients as appropriate and reasonable. Practices that generate larger average case fees, such as endodontists, periodontists, oral surgeons, and prosthodontists, may choose to charge interest after 90 days instead of 60.

In the event the account has gone over 60 days from date of treatment and the balance or a portion of the balance is covered by insurance on which you are accepting assignment of benefits, interest should be allowed to accumulate until the insurance has paid and then adjusted off the account. This should not be an issue for your office, because fewer than 2% of the insurance claims will not be paid within 60 days of the date of treatment, assuming the office is handling insurance appropriately.

The rate of interest I recommend is 1 1/2% per month or 18% per year.

There was no scientific formula used to come up with this rate. It is merely the rate that works best for my clients. If you were to charge a rate of 6% or 8% or 10%, which is lower than the rates that are commercially available through banks, credit unions, or VISA, then you might as well charge no interest at all. Your patients will have very little incentive to pay you off quickly. Eighteen percent is the rate that creates the fewest negative comments and provides the most positive result.

As with offering a discount, I do not pretend to give legal advice. Although I strongly encourage my clients to charge interest, your decision should be based on your personal philosophy in this matter combined with any applicable state or local regulations.

Charging Interest: Orthodontics

I do not recommend that orthodontists charge interest. Although I do not consider there to be any legal, moral, or ethical reasons not to do so, interest is not universally charged by orthodontists as it is by other dental specialities. In any event, since services are being provided over an extended period of time, an orthodontic office does not have the same incentive to encourage patients to pay at the time treatment is started as do other types of dental practices.

Summary

Interest is charged not for the income the interest generates, but solely as an inducement for patients to pay in the shortest period of time. Used in conjunction with a discount for payment at the time of treatment, you will find that an interest charge will be a powerful tool to encourage your patients to pay promptly.

CHAPTER 9

ACCEPTING CREDIT CARDS

I strongly encourage our clients to offer their patients the opportunity to use their VISA, MasterCard, American Express, or Discover cards to pay for their dental charges *if that is a method that the patients choose.* It is rare that I go into a doctor's office that is not already offering credit cards as a payment option. It is rarer still that I see more than 1% of the doctor's gross production being paid through the use of credit cards — in spite of the fact that the doctor may have signs in the reception area advising that he accepts credit cards.

As with the signs encouraging payment at the time of treatment, I will most often dispose of credit card signs and related materials in the office. In spite of this, our clients are successful in tripling and quadrupling the amount of their gross production paid with credit cards. This is because, historically, dental office staffs have not verbally offered their patients the opportunity to pay for treatment with their credit cards, and I encourage the staffs to present this option.

How to Present the Credit Card Option

Let me explain what I mean by "offering the patient the opportunity to pay with a credit card" as opposed to "suggesting" or "encouraging" patients to pay with a credit card. Remember from previous chapters the damage that can be done to referral rates and future growth of a practice by having aggressive financial policies? Aggressive policies include encouraging your patients to pay in any particular way for their dental care.

Use of credit cards for payment of dental care should be offered whenever the staff hears key words or key comments from patients: for instance, "I forgot my checkbook." Such a statement might generate the response from the receptionist: "Mrs. Jones, if you would like, you may use a credit card to pay for your charges." I suggest that no stronger effort than this be made to collect for the day's charges. Each of the administrative staff should be open to and aware of the key words and the key statements that make offering payment by credit card appropriate. They should waste no time in offering the use of that card whenever an appropriate situation arises.

Another effective time to suggest that a debt be paid with a credit card is when conducting collection activity. Virtually all credit card companies will allow telephone charges. If you are working with a patient who is temporarily unable to pay a past-due bill or a past-due payment or a number of payments in a manner that you desire, it is certainly appropriate that you suggest to that patient that he or she may want to pay by credit card over the phone. If you get the card number, the expiration date, and do a telephone authorization, this is a powerful way of reducing delinquency.

Dental Credit Cards

There are a number of dental credit card companies available to the dental practitioner today. Although each of these companies has slightly different policies and procedures, the end result is essentially the same: the dental office is not financing the dental care — the credit card company is. The patient is not paying the doctor monthly payments; he is paying the credit card company.

If you do not go into depth, this can sound like a pretty good deal. The patient is allowed financial arrangements over a longer period of time than the doctor would be willing to provide. The doctor gets his money up front. That sounds like a win-win in anybody's book. However, in practice, that is not quite the case.

I have evaluated offices that have used these card companies quite heavily, and invariably I find that the patients who use dental credit cards have little loyalty to that particular dental practice. They do not become long-term members of the practice. For instance, in one office the rate of no-show/last-minute cancels in the hygiene department among patients who paid with a dental credit card was *triple* that of patients using more conventional means of payment. I am convinced this is because patients who use these dental credit cards do not have the same relationship with the practice as those do who are making payments directly to the doctor's office or those who paid in full.

If a patient using a dental credit card misses a payment or must pay less than he had agreed to, he has to call a "collector" who may not even be in the same city as the patient. The patient cannot deal with a compassionate financial secretary who is willing to work with him. He must deal with an impersonal individual hundreds of miles away.

There are other problems which are less significant but should be mentioned. Quite often the doctor is required to accept payment at a discount on these credit cards — 5% to 10% is the most common. The patient pays an interest rate if 21% or even higher.

Factoring Companies

I find there are basically four types of dental practices. One is a practice that is liberal in granting credit, one is aggressive or restrictive in granting credit, another, which I call the "middle-of-the-road" practice, falls between the first two, and the fourth type is the practice that has chosen to "bail out" of handling credit management and accounts receivable control in the practice. This "bail out" is accomplished by utilizing the services of an organization known as a factoring company, although these companies will rarely present themselves to their potential customers as being factoring companies.

The way a factoring company operates is very simple. They come into a practice and purchase — write a check for — the existing receivables. This provides the practice with a tremendous cash windfall that can be used to pay off practice debt, purchase new equipment, expand the facilities, or fund a pension plan. (Sounds pretty good so far, doesn't it?) In addition, the factoring company will purchase your receivables on a weekly, bi-weekly, or monthly basis. They will actually write a check for the production over a given time period. (Sounds even better, doesn't it?) The patients now can make their payments over extended periods of time to a third-party organization. In fact, they can make payments over a longer period of time than the doctor would be willing to allow. (Sound like Utopia?) Utilizing a factoring company, the doctor's office no longer has to have a financial secretary to handle collection activity, billing, or questions from patients regarding their accounts, payment posting, etc. (It gets better!) To top it off, there are factoring companies that will throw in, free of charge, a computer which will keep track of the patients, give management reports, help with marketing, and speed up transmission of funds to the doctor's office from the factoring company. (Now you know you have died and gone to heaven!)

You might want to ask, "What's the catch?" Not only is there a "catch," but there are quite a few of them.

The Truth About Factoring Companies

First of all, a factoring company has to make a profit. That profit is made in a number of different ways. They purchase the receivables, and they purchase monthly production. But that production and those receivables are purchased at a discount. In other words, the doctor is not paid at face value but is paid a discounted amount — normally 88–94% of face value. All of a sudden that free computer isn't free anymore, is it? The average factoring company charges a 7% to 8% discount.

Suppose a doctor is willing to pay 8% of his gross each month in return for the benefit of getting a computer, having receivables purchased, and not carrying receivables. After all, it was costing $200 or $300 a month to send statements; it was costing $1,500 a month for a financial secretary; and the doctor was seriously considering spending $20,000 on a computer anyway. So, an 8% discount doesn't seem too expensive. Let's look further.

Month one rolls around and the doctor gets a check from the factoring company for 92% of his gross. The 8% hit is tough to take, but the doctor didn't like that financial secretary anyway, and the computer sure is nice. Second month, another 92%. Third month, another 92%. His budget is adjusted now to collecting 92% of his gross revenue. In fact, as it turns out, that is no better than he was averaging before he went to the factoring company. He has less overhead and more net income, so things are fine. All of a sudden, the fourth month rolls around, and the check, instead of being 92% of his gross, is 89%. With a quick phone call to the factoring company, the doctor discovers that not only do they take an 8% discount, but all of his old accounts, all of his old receivables, and all of his current production are purchased on "full recourse." The doctor has signed a recourse contract. A quick check with the dictionary, and the doctor learns that "full recourse" means he agrees to buy back any accounts that do not pay the factoring company.

The factoring company may have explained this to the doctor at the time he originally signed the contract. But in the euphoria of seeing a $50,000 or $60,000 check for his receivables and a guaranteed 92% of his gross each month, he did not dwell on the subject. The factoring company representative probably assured the doctor they had a staff of collection personnel who were very good at what they did and would be able to maintain delinquency at extremely low and certainly acceptable levels.

Another month rolls around and the doctor's check is 85%. Another contact with the factoring company, and he finds out that since his production had gone up recently (perhaps due to a fee increase) his "reserves" were not sufficient. The factoring company, therefore, was taking funds from the doctor's current production to fund his reserve account. With more research he finds out that the factoring company maintains this reserve account to protect themselves in the event the doctor should default in his agreement with them.

All of a sudden the doctor realizes he is only collecting 85% of his gross, and his net income is getting uncomfortably close to what it was before he went to the factoring company.

A few months after starting with the factoring company, the doctor notices an alarming increase in his no-show/cancellation rate in hygiene. In addition, he finds his case acceptance rate is declining among the patients he is still seeing. He questions a few of his patients and finds they are unhappy paying a third-party organization that may be thousands of miles away from the office. Further, they are unhappy dealing with a collection person who does not have the same empathy they felt the financial secretary had.

Essentially, the doctor is seeing a deterioration in the well-being of his practice. He comes to the conclusion that he has made a mistake — that the benefits of a factoring company do not make up for the disadvantages. The doctor decides that he will no longer send the factoring company his receivables; that he will carry his own accounts once again. Immediately he notices two things.

First of all, he has no more receivables. There is no cushion to provide cash flow to the practice on a daily, weekly, and monthly basis. Since it is necessary that some patients make monthly payments on the care that the doctor provides, his cash flow for the next three to six months (until he builds his receivables back up to appropriate levels) is going to be quite poor. So he goes to the bank and gets a bank loan for operating expenses to pull himself through. The next day he opens his mail and finds a demand letter from the factoring company advising him that according to the terms of his agreement he cannot stop selling his production to them unless he buys back his receivables, and they are presenting a bill for an additional $40,000 or $50,000.

Summary

You can see from this scenario (which was taken from an actual case study of one of our clients) that participation with a factoring company can cause very significant, long-term problems for the health care practice. I would like to add here that factoring companies are not inherently bad organizations. I have no evidence that they are actively dishonest or deceitful or are in any way practicing anything that is unlawful. Quite the contrary, factoring companies have been around for years and are commonly used by small and mid-size businesses to purchase their short-term receivables. In that environment, a factoring company can provide a valued service. It is highly inappropriate, however, for the health care community.

CHAPTER 10

MAKING FINANCIAL AGREEMENTS

Basically, all conversations regarding the patient's fee for services can be put into two categories: financial discussions (FD's) and financial arrangements (FA's). It is important to keep in mind, though, that there is a vast difference in the nature of these two categories, and, therefore, different skills and approaches are required to successfully conduct each conversation. Let's explore the nature of a financial discussion (FD) first.

The Financial Discussion

A financial discussion is a conversation with the patient regarding payment for services *after* they have been performed. Most commonly, this conversation is done at the front counter as the patient is dismissed from the operatory. The financial discussion is normally conducted on minor or routine treatment plans, usually in dollar amounts of $150 or less (routine prophies, exams, x-rays, minor amalgam restorations).

The verbal skills used in conducting a financial discussion are critical. Remember that you want to be paid for the treatment you have done. You would like to be paid today. *But*, damage could be done if you "require" that payment be made today.

Good verbal skills for a routine financial discussion might be: "Mrs. Smith, your charges were $140. If you would like to take care of that today, we could offer you a 5% discount." Notice the words "if you would like." These are key words in this conversation.

Two things are accomplished here: 1) The patient is advised of the day's charges, and 2) The patient is encouraged to pay today by offering a 5% discount. By the choice of words, "if you would like," what is unstated is that payment today is optional, and the patient can pay according to the terms as stated on the financial policy brochure (as described in Chapter 6 on presenting office policy).

If your staff uses these verbal skills with each patient receiving routine care, you will find an extremely high percentage of your patients will pay at the time of treatment. The majority of my clients find that the rate of patients paying in full for routine care does not decline due to the implementation of new, more lenient credit policies. In fact, my clients find the rate at least stays the same. The difference is that under the new credit policy, patients are paying because they choose to, not because they have to. Therefore, their attitude toward the office and toward the office's financial policies is much improved.

The Financial Arrangement

One of the primary differences between the financial arrangement and the financial discussion is that the financial arrangement is done with patients on a diagnosed treatment that has not yet been provided. Another difference is that financial arrangements are usually done on treatment that is not minor — treatment over $150. (You will find, however, that financial arrangements will be conducted from time to time even on minor treatment plans with your "B" and "C" patients.)

Conducting a financial arrangement is not as simple as having a conversation with a patient about how he is going to pay for the diagnosed care. You need to consider 1) when to make the financial arrangement, 2) where to make the financial arrangement, 3) who should make the financial arrangement, and 4) what verbal skills should be used in making the financial arrangement.

Let's look more closely at each of these items in order to learn what steps can be taken in order to make a high-quality financial arrangement.

Remember that the purpose of a financial arrangement is not simply to ensure that you get paid for the completed work. The primary purpose for a financial arrangement is to sell your treatment plan; that is, to sell the work that has been diagnosed. Most dentistry that has been diagnosed but not accepted by patients is not accepted because of the patient's financial considerations. Most of these considerations are based on misconceptions about how that practice *might* handle money. A clear financial arrangement which lets the patient know you are willing to work with him to see he gets the dentistry he needs will give you a tremendous boost in your case acceptance percentage.

The second goal is to ensure that you are paid for the work that has been diagnosed. An analysis of any doctor's receivables and delinquency quickly will show that most delinquency is not a result of a practice full of "deadbeat" patients or poor collection activity. Quite the contrary, most delinquency is the result of poor credit management policies in the office, which lead to poor quality or nonexistent financial arrangements made with the patients.

Keeping these two goals in mind — selling the case and getting an agreement about money — let's get into the details. First things being first, we should consider:

> *1. When to make the financial arrangement.* As commercial as this may seem, most dentistry is elective. If you accept the fact that the diagnosed care is most often elective and that it is the practice's desire that this care be provided, then conducting a financial arrangement is, in fact, "closing the sale."

When you are making a financial arrangement, you are trying to get the patient to purchase what you are selling. I warned you that this was somewhat commercial! But, if you are willing to take a pragmatic look at the business you are in, you will recognize there is quite a bit of sales work involved.

A financial arrangement should be done as soon as possible and whenever you have a patient who is willing to have a financial arrangement made. If you have a major treatment plan to present and you have a patient who is willing to have a financial arrangement made, do not postpone that financial arrangement until you have time to mount x-rays, or put study models on an articulator. The same is true in orthodontics. In my opinion, it is foolish to force a patient who does not need or want a formal case presentation to come back for one when all he wants to know is how much treatment costs and how he can pay for it.

In the vast majority of cases, financial arrangements should always be made on the same day care has been diagnosed. Often that will not be possible because some patients will want to discuss the treatment or finances with a spouse and other patients will want to "think about it." Firm financial arrangements should be conducted on 50–75% of all treatment plans on the date the treatment has been diagnosed. Many of your patients will not be ready to make a financial arrangement on the date treatment has been diagnosed. For a number of different reasons, making a firm financial arrangement on that date will not be convenient or appropriate. Therefore, make it a policy to set a time and a place for making financial arrangements *prior to the time* the treatment is provided.

The financial secretary should review the appointment schedule daily to ensure that all patients scheduled for the next day have had money properly handled. If the financial secretary discovers that a scheduled patient has not made financial arrangements, certainly she should contact the patient and conduct a financial arrangement by telephone. With this policy, the financial arrangement can be written out and ready for the patient to sign upon his arrival in the office the next day.

The third and least acceptable method of conducting a financial arrangement is on the day of the treatment, prior to the time the patient goes into the operatory for treatment. This policy is least acceptable because you have very little latitude. There will be pressures from the doctor and from the appointment secretary to keep the schedule full, and the appointment secretary likely will be unwilling to postpone treatment and leave a gaping hole in the schedule just because the patient was unable to make a financial arrangement that the financial secretary felt was appropriate. This puts an unnecessary burden on the financial secretary, and except in unusual circumstances, this situation should never be allowed to occur.

The policy of making financial arrangements on major treatment plans after the work has been provided is entirely unacceptable. An interview with any financial secretary will quickly uncover the result of this policy: high delinquency and an even higher level of frustration and dissatisfaction.

2. Where a financial arrangement should be made. The worst possible place in your office for making a financial arrangement is the front counter. Financial arrangements made at the front counter will invariably generate weaker case acceptance and higher delinquency among those who do accept the case. If you are conducting financial arrangements at your front counter, your patients will feel rushed and uncomfortable. Other staff members are coming and going as are other patients. In addition, there are other interruptions such as ringing telephones. With the combination of extraneous activity and little or no confidentiality, financial arrangements conducted at the front counter will be weak at best.

The second worst place to conduct financial arrangements is in the operatory. The dental chair, while designed very efficiently to support the clinical aspect of dentistry, was never designed to support the administrative side of dentistry. There is absolutely no way your patient will ever be comfortable making a financial arrangement seated in the dental chair.

In most offices this leaves only one place to make a financial arrangement: a private office, preferably a consultation room designed for that purpose. If your office does not have a consultation room but does have an office for the doctor, then I would suggest that the doctor give up his office and make it into a consultation room or that his office serve both purposes. Financial arrangements conducted in a private, quiet consultation room will be less rushed and will give the patient the opportunity to communicate his feelings and to ask questions, whether those questions are clinical or financial.

3. Who should make the financial arrangement? As with the "where," I would like to answer this by saying who should not: the doctor. In fact, the doctor should *never* make the financial arrangement. If it needs to be more clear, the doctor should never, under any conditions, for any reason, make a financial arrangement with a patient even if that means that the financial arrangement will be postponed because there is not another human being in the office to make the financial arrangement.

The very parts of a doctor's personality or character that make him a good health care provider are the very same aspects of his personality that make him the person who should never be discussing money with his patients. The doctor will invariably "sell the farm" when he discusses money with his patients. It is extremely rare and unusual that a doctor will ever be able to take a pragmatic look at the patient's true situation and make a financial arrangement that is appropriate for the patient and best for the overall well-being of the practice. More often than not, the doctor will make a decision based on emotion, rather than on factual information.

Even if the doctor were able to take a practical look at the patient — and I suppose I would agree that there are a few doctors who could do a good job — it would still be inappropriate, because the financial secretary would never have the ability to control that patient in the future. Since the doctor made the financial arrangement originally, it would be the doctor to whom the patient would go if he ever had a problem. It would be impossible to transfer that relationship back to the financial secretary where it belongs. I require my clients to take an oath written in blood, "I promise that under no conditions will I ever discuss money with my patients!"

As to who should make the financial arrangement, the obvious answer is the financial secretary, but that is not necessarily the correct answer. Although the financial secretary certainly can make the financial arrangement, in many client offices, persons other than the financial secretary make the financial arrangement because patient flow dictates that a treatment coordinator, PR person, or other employee do the job. This is acceptable and in many cases it is desirable. If I were a doctor, deciding who in my office would make the financial arrangement, the job would be given to the best salesperson because my goal is having my case sold.

A good treatment coordinator (PR person) will have as a primary goal selling the case that has been presented to the patient. Another important goal will be to obtain a financial agreement with the patient that is beneficial to the practice. This leads us to the final item to consider when making the financial arrangement.

4. What verbal skills to use when presenting a financial arrangement. Your practice has done a lot of work so far. You have done internal or external marketing of one kind or another in order to attract the patient to the practice. You have designed an efficient scheduling system to get the patient into the practice for his new patient exam. Appropriate documentation has been completed on the new patient. The patient has been seated in the clinical chair, examined by the doctor, and had work diagnosed. A tremendous amount of effort, time, and expense has gone into getting the patient this far into the relationship. Now it is up to the person making the financial arrangement not to "blow it." Her job is to see to it that the patient accepts the care that has been diagnosed.

5. With whom should financial arrangements be made? Certainly everybody agrees that a financial arrangement should be made on a patient new to the practice who has had significant amounts of treatment diagnosed. But what about your brother-in-law or the hygienist's sister? What about the minister and his wife or other members of "our church"? What about your fraternity brother or next door neighbor? What about good old Mr. and Mrs. Smith who have been in your practice for 20 years? Certainly you don't need to make a financial arrangement with them, do you? The answer is "yes" to all of the above. Remember that a true and absolute commitment to quality is rarely comfortable. And although it may be uncomfortable to make a financial arrangement with your best friend or "good old Mr. and Mrs. Smith," if you want to serve your patients and have the best possible relationship with those patients, if you want to sell an optimum amount of dentistry, and if you want to be paid in the manner that is most appropriate for the well-being of the practice, then a financial arrangement needs to be made with each patient who has had any significant treatment diagnosed.

There is a test of this policy that will determine whether or not a financial arrangement needs to be made with any given patient. The test is: Are you willing to do this work for free? Are you willing to conduct absolutely no collection activity? Are you willing to write the account off as uncollectible and continue to provide ongoing additional progressive care for this patient? If the answer to all of these questions is "yes," then it is not necessary for you to make a financial arrangement with that particular patient.

Remember the two main goals: 1) sell the case and 2) get the best possible financial arrangement. There are five steps that the financial secretary or treatment coordinator can follow to optimize the chances of fulfilling those two goals in an excellent manner. These five steps are as follows: 1) prepare, 2) try for payment in full, 3) negotiate a down payment, 4) negotiate a monthly payment and a due date, and 5) review the terms of the agreement and sign an appropriate financial agreement document.

1. *Prepare.*

a. Evaluate the patient. Review the patient history form. Be certain it is complete in every detail, and make the ABC decision. Obtain a credit report on the patient and use the information contained therein to support or perhaps change the credit decision that was based on the patient history form alone.

b. Estimate insurance. Do not "guesstimate" insurance. Review your insurance log. If that information is not available, pick up the phone and get the information needed. The financial secretary will not be able to sell this case unless she is able to accurately estimate insurance coverage.

c. Establish her limits; that is, set parameters. How far is she willing to negotiate with this patient? Is this an "A+" patient to whom she is willing to give virtually unlimited credit? No down payment? Six months to pay? Is this a "B+" patient where a very large down payment is minimally acceptable and she is willing to finance the balance over one to three months? Or is this a "C" patient for whom she will have no parameters because she will require cash only for any additional work?

It is important that limits be established *prior* to the time that the financial secretary has any conversation with the patient. Decisions she makes while in conversation with the patient may be based on emotion rather than based on a practical evaluation of the patient and his situation. For this reason, the credit evaluation is made and the financial arrangement limits are established prior to the time the financial secretary sits down with the patient. Remember that when the financial secretary establishes these limits, she should establish the lowest down payment and the lowest monthly payment she is willing to accept. She is stating her absolute limit. In other words, she would be willing to lose the patient rather than make a financial arrangement that does not fall within the guidelines. This does not mean that she necessarily is going to make financial arrangements that are this liberal. She is going to use good verbal skills and complete the following steps which will make it infrequent that she will ever have to negotiate to the limits she has established. But since some limits are needed with virtually every patient, those limits must be established prior to the time she sits down with the patient.

It is important to note that the financial secretary is the one and only person who should be performing step one of the financial arrangement. She is the only person who will be trained and qualified to make the ABC decisions and to establish the financial limits for the patient that will be best for the practice. Once step one has been properly completed by a well-trained and committed financial secretary, then the parameters can be presented to any staff member (for instance, a treatment coordinator or PR person) to conduct the financial arrangement. Many of our clients have found that the patient flow is smoother and case acceptance is better when a person who is not the financial secretary actually makes the financial arrangement. I have just as many client practices, however, where all financial arrangements are made by the financial secretary. Both systems can be made to work well as long as the financial secretary is responsible for actually establishing the credit limits. Once the financial secretary has established the patient's credit rating and the negotiation parameters that will be used (step one of the financial arrangement), the treatment coordinator or other appropriate person can handle the financial arrangement. If the person making the financial arrangement will follow the suggestions below, it will be a rare case that she will ever have to negotiate down to the limits set by the financial secretary.

2. *Try for payment in full.* I am always amazed at the number of practices in which the doctor and/or his staff make an assumption that just because the cost of treatment is substantial, the patients automatically need financial arrangements to pay for it. This assumption prevents one from making the first attempt to collect the case fee in full. If the financial arranger makes a commitment to ask each time, no matter how poor or destitute a patient may appear, you will be amazed with the results.

By now it should be clear to your patient that your practice is prepared to offer financial arrangements. He has read your brochure which indicates that "financial arrangements are available upon special request" (see Chapter 6 — Presenting The Office Policy). Therefore, the first offer to your patient is an inducement for payment in full. I recommend a 5% discount (10% for orthodontics). As in the financial discussion at the front counter, make it clear to the patients that you are not pushing them into paying for treatment in advance.

The verbal skills would be: "Mrs. Smith, the crown the doctor has diagnosed will be $500. If you would like to take care of that today or at any time up to the day we start treatment, we would be pleased to offer a 5% discount." Again, notice the "If you would like . . ." Certainly the "A" and "B" patient has an option in this respect. Since the "C" patient has no option, the verbal skills used in making financial arrangements will be much more direct: "Mrs. Smith, the fee for the treatment the doctor has diagnosed is $500 which will be due on or before the day treatment is started."

A very successful tool in any sales effort is the "strategic pause." A strategic pause is a break in the conversation at a point where a break is not expected. For example, when presenting step two of a financial arrangement the treatment co-ordinator would say, "Mrs. Smith, the treatment is $500. If you would like to take care of that today or at any time up to the time we start treatment, we can offer you a 5% discount." At this point the financial secretary or treatment coordinator stops talking and waits for a response.

When step two is presented in this manner, there will be a quick response from the patient. The response will vary from, "Why, yes, certainly, I will be glad to pay it and take advantage of the discount," to "There is no possibility of my paying it in full," or "I may be able to do it. Do I have any other options?" The astute treatment coordinator will recognize that any answer other than "Yes" is "No." That negative response may also take the form of, "Yes, I think I can do that. However, I need to check with my husband first." This is nothing more complicated than a negative response to her suggestion, and she needs to be willing to go to the next step.

One of the most important parts of presenting a financial arrangement appropriately is to remember that the financial arranger must never go from one step to another until she has gotten an answer concerning the step that she is in. For instance, she would not go into step three, a discussion of the down payment, until she has some kind of definitive answer to step two.

An example of how step two could be presented inappropriately would be, "Mrs. Smith, your treatment will be $500. If you would like to take care of that today or at any time up to the time we start treatment we can offer you a 5% discount, or we could set you up on a monthly payment plan." Certainly you can see the problem with this type of presentation. You have given the patient a choice, and the patient will very likely want to reserve judgment on which decision she will make until after she has heard both of the choices. The natural response would be, "What type of financial arrangements can I make?"

If the patient has, in one way or another, declined the offer in step two, then the financial arranger would move on to step three.

3. *Negotiate a down payment.* When payment in full is not obtained, the financial arranger still recognizes that her obligation is to get the largest down payment reasonable, keeping in mind her goal of making sure the patient accepts the diagnosis. In a conversation about down payment, there will be no conversation about monthly payments. The verbal skills may be: "Mrs. Smith, since this is major treatment, we would like to have a down payment of $250." The language of "We would like to have . . ." lets the patient know there is another option, but the amount she is suggesting is something that she considers to be appropriate and within the patient's means. In most cases this approach will be successful in obtaining the down payment asked for. If the patient is reluctant to pay the down payment requested, the financial arranger can continue to negotiate the amount downwards until she has reached the limits established in step one. In no event will she ever negotiate a down payment that is less than the limits established previously. Remember, any decision made at this point is likely to be based on emotion rather than facts and, therefore, will be inappropriate.

I want to take a moment here to define what is meant by the term "down payment." A down payment is that amount of money paid "down" on or before the date care is provided. It is important that this definition be understood. If the financial secretary has determined that a "B+" patient must have a minimum down payment of $500 and the patient advises that she will pay $250 now and $250 in three weeks, then treatment must be postponed until the entire $500 is received. A down payment may not be split up unless the amount received, on or before the date care is provided, is equal to or greater than the minimum limit set by the financial secretary.

Let's take another example. Patient Jones is an "A+" patient; the financial secretary has determined that no down payment is necessary to start treatment. In the actual financial arrangement, however, Mr. Jones promises to pay $300 down today and $300 in a week with monthly payments of $100 for six months. Can you start Mr. Jones' treatment today? Certainly you can because you would have started him without any down payment, so a split down payment is perfectly acceptable. If, however, Mr. Jones were a "B" patient and the financial secretary had determined that $600 was the minimum down payment acceptable, then Mr. Jones would have to wait until he paid the entire $600 before he could start treatment.

Once she has negotiated a down payment acceptable to the practice and to the patient, it is time to go on to step four.

4. *Negotiate a monthly payment and a due date.* The verbal skills for this may be: "After a down payment of $200, the balance of your account would be $300. I could set that up in two monthly payments of $150 each. Would that work for you?" Again, her initial offer to the patient is a financial arrangement that is best for the practice and may or may not fit the patient's particular situation. If that monthly payment is inappropriate or unacceptable to the patient, she will surely tell you. In any event, the financial arranger will negotiate with the patient until an agreement is reached on a monthly payment amount and for how many months. As in step three, the financial arranger will not negotiate the monthly payment any lower than the minimum established in step one.

The second part of step four is establishing the due date. It is very common in the health care profession for doctors' offices to establish due dates that are in conjunction with their statement dates or their billing dates. I have always felt this was foolish. In virtually all health care practices, patients pay when they want to throughout the month. Pay dates have little to do with the doctor's billing date. However, they have everything to do with your patients' paydays. It is, therefore, appropriate that you recognize this fact and ask the patient what an appropriate due date would be. The verbal skills may sound like this: "Mrs. Smith, what day of the month is most convenient for you to make your payments?" Any day that the patient chooses should be acceptable to your office.

Step five of the financial arrangement is, along with step one, a most crucial step.

5. *Review the terms of the agreement and sign an appropriate financial agreement document.* While the financial arranger is reviewing the financial arrangement verbally with the patient, she should be filling in the blanks of a financial agreement form (see Fig. 10–1).

The verbal skills could sound like this: "We have agreed then, Mrs. Smith, that the fee for the treatment is $500, and you will make an initial payment of $200 due on the date care is provided. The balance of $300 will be paid in three equal payments of $100 each with the first payment due on April 15 and subsequent installments on the same date the next two months. Is that correct?"

Once she has thoroughly reviewed the financial agreement with the patient and once she has gotten the affirmative answer to her final question, it is appropriate that the patient (or the responsible party) sign the financial agreement. When the patient signs the form, your financial arranger has just sold a case and made a quality financial agreement.

To summarize, it is imperative that you recognize the primary purpose for a financial arrangement. It is not to make sure you collect your fee for the treatment you are about to render, although that is certainly a secondary and very desired result. The primary purpose for a financial arrangement is to "sell" the case. Dentistry is elective, and in most cases your patients can choose whether or not to receive the care you have diagnosed. In addition, your patients can choose to have the care provided by you, or they can choose to have it provided by another doctor down the street. So a financial arrangement is, in fact, a very powerful way to "close the sale."

In concluding this chapter, I ask you to remember that financial arrangements do not have to be looked upon as negative or as uncomfortable for your patients. If the right approach is taken, and if the right verbal skills are used, a financial arrangement can be an extremely positive experience for both you and your patient. The patient will leave your office with a strong sense of satisfaction. He will be aware of your concern for his well-being and your consideration for his needs, and his relationship with the practice will be enhanced. Your staff has sold a case, and your chances of promptly being paid have been optimized. Your relationship with the patient is enhanced which will generate more case acceptance in the future and better referral rates.

This document does not meet and is not intended to meet the guidelines established by Regulation Z of the Uniform Commercial Code known as the Truth-in-Lending Law. There has been tremendous discussion and dissension

FINANCIAL AGREEMENT

Dr. John Jones
2270 N.W. 124th St.
Portland, OR 97229

FOR PROFESSIONAL SERVICES Rendered or to be Rendered:

Responsible Party (1) ______________________________

Patient (2) ______________________________

Treatment covered by this agreement (3) ______________________________

____

1. Professional Fee $ (4) ________
2. Less **Estimated** Insurance $ (5) ________
3. Less Cash Down Payment $ (6) ________ Due: (7) ________
4. Unpaid Balance $ (8) ________

Unpaid balance (#4 above) is payable to (9) ________ in (10) ________ monthly installments of $ (11) ________ each, and (12) ________ installments of $ (13) ________ each, the first installment being payable on (14) ________ 19________, and subsequent installments on the same day of each consecutive month until paid in full. 1½% per month interest (18% per year) will be charged on accounts 60 days from treatment date.

(15) ________________ Date

(17) ________________ Signature

(16) ________________ Witness

Zuelke & Associates 1988 ©

Fig. 10–1

in the legal community about whether or not it is necessary for a doctor who makes a financial arrangement with a patient for medical or dental treatment to follow the guidelines of the Truth-in-Lending Regulations. My personal opinion is that these regulations are so complex and the rules are so specific, it is almost impossible for a health care practice interested in providing health care to its patients to follow the Regulation Z guidelines. For instance, under the guidelines, you are required to call your case fee or professional fee a "Cash Price."

The form in Figure 10–1 is the document currently used by the majority of clients throughout the country. Again, it does not comply and is not intended to comply with Truth-in-Lending Regulations although it does follow the intent of these regulations in disclosing the specific terms of the agreement in as accurate a manner as possible.

1. The name of the responsible party or parties (not necessarily the patient).

2. The name of the patient who is going to receive the care for which a financial arrangement is being made.

3. The actual care you intend to provide for the fee listed, itemized as accurately as possible.

4. The gross case fee before any adjustments or discounts.

5. The *estimated* amount of gross case fee (item 4.) that will be covered by dental insurance.

6. Down payment.

7. Date when down payment will be due.

8. Item 4. minus item 5. minus item 6.

9. The name of the doctor or organization providing the health care

10. The number of monthly payments agreed to minus one (For instance, if there is a six-month financial arrangement agreed to, then 5 would be entered in this item.

11. The amount of the monthly payment that has been agreed to.

12. One.

13. The words "the balance" (For instance, properly completed it would read, "Unpaid balance (item 4. above) is payable to Dr. James Smith in six monthly installments of $100 each and one installment of the balance.")

Note: Items 10., 11., 12., and 13. are handled in this manner because with interest charged on the unpaid balance it is not possible to accurately determine the exact amount of the final payment. In addition, it is likely that this patient or a member of his immediate family may come in and receive additional care prior to the time this financial arrangement is paid in full.

14. The due date has been agreed to in step 4 of the financial arrangement.

15. The date that financial agreement took place.

16. Witnessed by the office employee conducting the financial arrangement.

17. Signed by a financially responsible party as identified in item 1.

CHAPTER 11

PROCESSING INSURANCE CLAIMS

Currently there is tremendous controversy in the dental profession: Is it or is it not appropriate or necessary to accept assignment of insurance benefits? Before I discuss this issue, I want to state my definition of acceptance of insurance assignment: The dental practice quotes a fee to a patient, determines how much of that fee is likely to be covered by dental insurance, and either collects the patient's portion or makes a financial arrangement on the portion that is not covered by insurance. If the office policy is to make a financial arrangement on the entire case fee and then bill the insurance for the patients, that is *not* accepting assignment of insurance benefits.

Common Objections

When I present this issue in a seminar, or even in my private client offices, I often face a storm of protest from all sides. Some doctors protest with the comment: "Why should I have to wait for my money? It is the patient's insurance; it is his benefit. He should pay me and collect from his own insurance." Or, "Insurance takes far too long to pay. We have claims that are months old and still have not paid." From the administrative staff I hear: "It is impossible to accurately estimate insurance coverage. It is too much paperwork, and we don't have the time."

I am amazed that so much controversy could surround a procedure that can have such a tremendous positive impact on the well-being of the practice. Certainly, there is additional paperwork and additional workload associated with maintaining appropriate insurance records and conducting insurance follow-up, but I ask my clients to think of what they are accomplishing as a trade-off for all of that additional work.

The Benefits

Improved cash flow/higher case acceptance. In any office, some patients are willing to pay in full and bill their own insurance. Others, of course, will have to make financial arrangements on the fee for their treatment and may be willing to make a financial arrangement based on the entire case fee, even though they have insurance. To enhance cash flow, you must be willing to accurately estimate insurance coverage and make a financial arrangement with the patient on his portion of the fee. That financial arrangement would, of course, include an appropriate down payment and an appropriate monthly payment. Assuming the claim form is properly completed and promptly filed, you will receive the insurance benefits within 30 days of the date of treatment. In most cases, the end result is a higher cash flow for your office over that of the office making financial arrangements with the patient on the entire case fee.

When I compare offices that are equal, except one is accepting insurance assignment and one is not, I find the office that is accepting insurance assignment has significantly higher case acceptance. The reason is obvious: If a case for $2,000 is presented to a patient and the practice is willing to accept assignment of insurance benefits (in this case let's say insurance pays $1,000), the patient will be much more receptive to making a financial arrangement on the balance of $1,000 rather than on the total of $2,000.

Lower delinquency. By accepting assignment of insurance benefits, the typical dental office also has lower delinquency. If payment is received for the portion of the fee covered by insurance directly from an insurance company, there is less money in receivables or "on the books." Therefore, there is less potential delinquency.

Increased patient satisfaction. This is the most powerful outcome of accepting assignment of insurance benefits. There is no legal, moral, or ethical obligation to accept assignment of insurance benefits or even to file an insurance claim on a patient's behalf. But, how many claim forms per year does the average patient file on his own behalf? One or two perhaps? Patients have little experience and little knowledge of dental insurance and dental insurance companies. They are far more likely to make mistakes in filing, thus causing delays in payment. With hundreds of insured patients and dozens of insurance companies, the dental office is exposed to insurance to a greater degree and has the ability to accumulate information regarding various insurance companies more effectively than does an individual patient. The dental office has the experience to effectively deal with insurance companies on their patients' behalf and, therefore, increase the level of patient satisfaction with the practice. Anything the office can do to increase patient satisfaction — the quality of the relationship between the practice and the patient — is going to enhance the well-being of the practice. In earlier pages of this book, I stated that patients who are satisfied in their relationship with a practice are going to 1) accept more care, 2) give more and better referrals, 3) keep their agreements with the practice more readily, and 4) contribute in a positive way to the quality of life within the practice.

If by accepting assignment of insurance benefits, a practice will have lower delinquency, improved cash flow, higher case acceptance, and an overall higher level of patient satisfaction, then the astute dental office will find a way to overcome the real and perceived problems associated with acceptance of insurance benefits.

Before discussing problems associated with insurance, I would like to clarify the three types of third-party payers that typically fall under the category of "Dental Insurance." It is imperative that the dental office staff recognize the nature of each and their differences. They are: 1) closed-panel or participating companies, 2) self-insured employer, and 3) the true dental insurance company. Let's look at closed-panel insurance companies first.

Closed-Panel

This type of company requires the doctor to sign a participatory agreement. It is usually in the form of a signed contract in which the doctor agrees to follow a certain set of rules and regulations and agrees to maintain fees at or below a certain level. In return, the insurance company agrees to list that doctor as one of a group of "participating" doctors. This list is available to the patients insured under this particular plan. Generally speaking, I am opposed to the idea of a participating plan, because I feel it is inappropriate for any insurance company, organization, or outside party to dictate to a doctor what his fees should be. I consider this to be the primary disadvantage of being a member of any participating plan.

There is reality to deal with, however, and there are many areas of the country (specifically, Michigan, Minnesota, and California) where the participating companies have such a large cross-section of the public as members of their plan, that refusal to participate may cause a serious erosion in the patient flow of the practice. My recommendation is not to participate with closed-panel organizations unless 25% or more of your potential patient flow is employed by firms utilizing the closed-panel companies.

Another disadvantage of dealing with participating companies is that under many participatory agreements, you often consent to follow procedures that can be disruptive to your practice. In fact, some procedures can diminish your case acceptance. For instance, some of these companies require that you use their claim form rather than the standard ADA or AAO approved claim form. This causes disruption in the paper flow of the practice, requiring you to keep separate sets of forms. This disruption usually results in a delay in getting insurance properly filed. This is a minor but, nevertheless, annoying situation.

Another agreement typically required by these plans is that you will file pre-authorizations on all treatment over a certain dollar amount. This may sound like a reasonable request except when you consider two problems. Problem #1: a pre-authorization requires additional paperwork. Problem #2: a pre-authorization obviously results in a delay in providing the dental care suggested to the patient. And, delay will invariably result in a lower level of case acceptance.

An Aside About Pre-Authorizations

A well-known dental consultant in a national survey determined that up to 50% of all general dental patients never come back to have diagnosed work done when pre-authorization has occurred. My own experience shows this figure to be a little high. But there is no doubt that at least 35% of patients subjected to pre-authorization will not be back to have the work done. Insurance companies will routinely tell you that the pre-authorizations are required for "cash flow planning," and for "patient comfort." I wouldn't be surprised if some insurance companies are not well aware that many patients with treatment pre-authorized never return to have the work done and, therefore, they save thousands or even millions of dollars per year in claims. That is purely speculation on my part.

Except when dealing with closed-panel companies and self-insured companies, I do not recommend pre-authorizations except in extremely rare cases (1 in 50). In fact, I actively instruct our clients to never pre-authorize except when it is impossible to estimate insurance coverage.

Many state insurance commissioners have determined that pre-authorizations cannot be required by insurance companies except closed-panel and self-insured employers. In other words an insurance company cannot refuse to pay an otherwise valid claim purely because it has not been pre-authorized. Do not be fooled by insurance claim forms printed by an insurance company or employer that has a statement, usually in block letters, "Claims over $__________ must be pre-authorized." If you are dealing with a regular insurance company (not one of the closed-panel companies and not an employer that is self-insured), a pre-authorization cannot be required before payment is rendered. A claim for appropriate services rendered will not be denied because you have not done a pre-authorization.

An additional problem, which may or may not be a problem in your particular area, is by being a member of a participating company you are required to maintain fees at or below a level established by the insurance company. By some mysterious formula insurance companies determine what are called "usual, customary, and reasonable" fees that are appropriate for your particular geographic area. You are not allowed to charge a fee to group members greater than this preset fee. With this type of plan, your fees or proposed fee increases must be submitted to the insurance company periodically "for approval." It is not unusual for me to travel to an area of the country where participating doctors are charging up to 25% less for their services than are non-participating doctors in the same community.

The only advantage that I can see to being a member of a participating plan is that in some areas of the country (such as those mentioned earlier) you will attract a larger new patient flow to the practice by being a member of the participating plan. The doctor has to decide which direction to take. Depending on your geographic location, this may be a tough choice, indeed.

Self-Insured Employer

The second type of organization is commonly referred to as an insurance company, but it is not an insurance company at all. Ten years ago there were very few self-insured companies, but there are increasing numbers today.

Very simply, an employer in this category insures itself. Rather than paying premiums to an insurance company and then having the insurance company pay the claims, an employer essentially withholds dental insurance premiums from the employees' paychecks and retains those premiums for purposes of paying claims. (These companies hope that the claims they pay will be less than the premiums they have retained and that they will save themselves the insurance company's profit.) Sometimes these self-insured companies process and pay the claims themselves. Other times they have insurance companies or other companies that administer benefit plans on a contractual basis and pay the claims. Sometimes — especially when an employer is having an insurance company administer their self-insured plan — it is difficult to tell whether or not a company is self-insured, although you can find out by asking.

There are only a few problems in dealing with these types of companies.

1. They will sometimes require their own claim form. Therefore, you cannot use the standard ADA or AAO approved form.

2. Since they are not insurance companies, they do not have to follow any set of rules, and they can very often take long periods of time to pay a valid claim.

3. A few of these companies will not pay claims directly to the doctor. Even with a properly signed insurance assignment, some companies pay all benefits directly to the patient.

4. These self-insured companies can require pre-authorizations with the inherent problems I discussed earlier.

True Dental Insurance Company

This is the company we are the most familiar with. In most states they make up 90% of all of the third-party payers.

Accepting Insurance Benefits: The Most Common Problems

The problems that I hear most commonly associated with insurance are: 1) too much paperwork; 2) insurance companies take too long to pay; 3) it is impossible to accurately estimate insurance coverage; 4) the insurance company pays the patient and then the patient won't pay us; and 5) if we accept insurance assignment we have to accept reduced fees from some companies. Let's deal with these individually.

"There is too much paperwork." While it is true there is paperwork involved with accepting insurance assignment, there is also paperwork involved if you don't accept it. Typically, even though an office does not accept insurance assignment, the staff still fills out and signs insurance forms on their patients' behalf. Therefore, the "additional" paperwork associated strictly with acceptance of assignment of benefits should be of little significance.

"Insurance takes too long to pay." Over the years, I have rarely documented a case where insurance companies arbitrarily extended the time it took to pay a claim. When I tracked a claim that was delayed more than 30 days from the date care was provided, the cause could be traced to the dental office itself. Quite often claims were improperly filed (sent to the wrong insurance company) or incorrectly filled out (you must learn to play the insurance company game; every single "t" must be crossed, every "i" dotted, every blank filled in properly), and there was little follow-up on that claim conducted by the dental office.

The majority of states have an insurance commissioner who dictates the time that is allowed for processing and payment of dental insurance claims. Almost all states allow insurance companies 30 days to pay a claim. There are even a few states where this time is limited to 21 days from the date the claim was filed. I have found very few instances where insurance companies do not actually pay their claims within the deadline period. The assumption, of course, is that the claim was properly and promptly filed, with the emphasis on the claim form being *perfectly* completed.

When I investigate client complaints about insurance payments taking too long, another common problem is tremendous delay in processing and mailing claim forms from the office. Some offices do not use the approved standardized claim forms and require their patients to bring in their own. When a patient forgets or chooses not to do so, rather than handling it, the office staff sits back and waits for the patient to bring in the form, with accompanying delays in mailing the claim for payment.

In other cases, offices hold up a claim on a small procedure because the patient is coming in to have additional work done. Typically, they do this in an effort to avoid "paperwork," but the end result for the office is a delay in payment.

To avoid such problems, proper administrative procedures need to be established in your office. I regularly find that handling insurance does not have a high enough priority. Therefore, insurance is not billed promptly. It is not uncommon to review an office that has provided treatment two or three weeks earlier and has not billed insurance because nobody in the office has "gotten around to it."

Occasionally, an insurance company will temporarily reject a claim and return it to the office with a request for additional information. If these requests for additional information are not promptly handled, it results in an even greater delay in being paid.

My recommendation is that insurance forms be properly completed and in the mail within one working day of the date care was provided. The same is true of requests for additional information from insurance companies.

Handling insurance properly requires an employee who is primarily responsible for the effective handling of insurance claims. This need not be this person's only job description, but it should be one of the primary duties.

"It is impossible to accurately estimate insurance coverage." Once in a while I come across an office where the staff is absolutely convinced that insurance companies conspire to keep that type of information (how much they are going to cover on any particular procedure) from the dental office. Such people have convinced themselves that it is impossible to obtain such information. Yet, invariably, I will have clients in that same town accurately estimating insurance coverage for all of their patients on a regular basis. The difference clearly is in the attitude of the individual. There are commercial services (such as the Trojan System in California) that provide, for a fee, information to dental offices regarding the details of various employers' insurance coverage policies. These companies have no direct ties to insurance companies. They get this information the same way our clients obtain the information: through research, follow-up, phone calls to insurance companies, phone calls to employers, review of dental benefit booklets, review of EOB (Explanation of Benefits), and a thorough review of benefit checks when they arrive in the practice. Although compilation of this information is somewhat time consuming, it is relatively easy if the practice is committed to obtaining the information.

My recommendation is that an office develop an "insurance log" (see Fig. 11–1). This log is maintained alphabetically by employer and is kept in a three-ring binder. The insurance log has a significant amount of information in a very simple format that will enable the person responsible for insurance in your office to accurately estimate insurance coverage as well as facilitate the processing and proper completion of the claim. Virtually every piece of information needed to properly file the claim is included on this form. Special procedures with any given company can be noted in the space provided at the bottom of the form. This space is also used to document items of interest; for instance, comments such as, "This insurance company usually pays in 35 days" or "will not pay for porcelain veneers" or "does not return x-rays." Again, anything of special interest should be noted.

If the insurance company pays by fee schedule as opposed to a percentage of usual, customary, reasonable charges (UCR), that fee schedule can be printed on the reverse of the form (obtain from the patient's benefits booklet).

GENERAL DENTAL INSURANCE COMPANY FILE

Employer____

Address____

City______________ State_______ Zip__________ Phone____________

Name of Insurance Clerk______________________

Date of Inquiry______________________________

Insurance Carrier______________________________

Address____

City______________ State_______ Zip__________ Phone____________

DEDUCTIBLE Yes______ No______ Amount ______________

CO-INSURANCE Yes______ No______

Do you pay for replacement of missing teeth Yes______ No______

Do you have an annual maximum Yes______ No______ Amount______

Do you require pre-authorization Yes______No______If over $______

Coverage by percentage:

__________% ______________________________

Maximum $ amount paid_____________________

__________% ______________________________

Maximum $ amount paid_____________________

__________% ______________________________

Maximum $ amount paid_____________________

__________% ______________________________

Maximum $ amount paid_____________________

Coverage by fee schedule Yes______ No______ Approx. % __________

Waiting period for major dental Yes______ No______ Time________

LIMITATIONS:

Fig. 11–1

ORTHODONTIC INSURANCE INFORMATION FORM

Employer Name: ______________________

Employer Address: ______________________

____

____

Contact: ______________________

Insurance Co: ______________________

Insurance Address: ______________________

____

____

Contact: ______________________

Date of Inquiry: ______________________

BENEFITS INFORMATION:

Lifetime Maximum: __________ Yearly Maximum: __________

Adult Coverage: __________ Dependent Age Limit: __________

Deductible: __________ One Time: ______ Yearly: ______

Payment Percentage: ______________________

Payment Schedule: ______________________

Monthly: ________ Quarterly: ________ Semi-Annual: ________

Coupons: __________ Form Submitted Monthly: __________

Requires Pre-Authorization: Yes __________ No __________

Additional Information:

____

____

____

____

____

____

____

____

____

____

____

Fig. 11–2

Again, compilation of this log takes time. You will not be able to develop an adequate insurance log overnight. However, once you agree that accepting assignment of insurance benefits will enhance the well-being of the practice (with respect to cash flow, case acceptance and patient satisfaction) and commit to accepting assignment of insurance benefits, this log can be developed a page at a time over a period of time and will be a real asset to your practice. If you think about it, how many pages will you have to develop? If yours is like most practices, the majority of patients with dental insurance work at 50 or fewer employers. While this may not be true in large urban practices, it is true for the majority of dental practices in this country. My personal experience with developing this information is that 15 minutes of telephone work will obtain all of the information you need to complete one page of the insurance log. Consequently, you have the information necessary to properly file and accept assignment of insurance benefits.

"The insurance companies pay the patient and the patient won't pay us." This is a common complaint and in some offices a significant cause of delinquency and ultimate loss to the practice. The question I am asked is, "What can I do about it?" The answer, unfortunately, is that you can do very little about it. Ultimately any insurance benefits paid belong to the patient, not to the practice. Your patients pay a premium for health care coverage, and because they are paying that premium, they are personally entitled to receive the insurance benefits. A quick review of the assignment of benefits that you ask your patients to sign will show that it uses the words, "I hereby authorize." This simply means that the insurance company *may* pay the doctor directly; however, they are not required to do so. As hard as it may be to accept, that money belongs to the patient if he receives the benefits directly from the insurance company. He can choose to spend that money and not pay you. This may not be morally correct, but it is legal.

So, what is the practical answer to the question, "What do I do if a patient receives his insurance benefits and doesn't pay us?" Quite simply, treat the account as you would any other delinquent patient who has failed to keep an agreement with you. Conduct regular, routine collection activity on that patient until the problem is resolved. If you have surrounded yourself with stable, quality "A" patients, you rarely will be faced with this problem. When you are, you will have little trouble collecting your account balance.

"If we accept assignment of insurance benefits, we have to accept reduced fees from some companies." This problem was dealt with in the section on closed-panel insurance. Again, in the majority of cases, you can charge and collect from your insured patients the exact fee you would charge and collect from your non-insured patients. The exception is, of course, the closed-panel companies. Whether you choose to participate with those particular companies should be a management decision based on the number of potential patients that would be attracted to your practice if you were participating or that you would lose to the practice if you were not participating.

Capitation Plans, PPOs, Etc.

There are other types of organizations that provide reimbursement to the dental practice other than regular insurance, closed-panel or participating insurance, and self-insured employers. They are capitation plans, preferred provider plans, and dental maintenance plans. I have a strong belief that these types of organizations can cause significant damage to the fee-for-service private practice dental office and that it is inappropriate to sign up with, or in any way participate with such plans. In many years of traveling throughout the country, I have seen most of these plans, and I have not seen a single plan that did not result in one or more of three situations that I consider to be unacceptable to the profession:

1. A reduced level of care to the patients involved.
2. Substantially reduced revenue for the practice.
3. Patients that were uncommitted to quality health care.

Insurance Follow-up

If you accept assignment of insurance benefits, it means accepting responsibility (up to a limit) to see to it that the insurance company pays you and pays you promptly. To that end, a follow-up system in your office will allow you to identify insurance companies that are tardy in paying.

Most offices develop a simple 1–31 file for use after a claim has been filed. With this system, a copy of the insurance or insurance continuation form is placed in a 1–31 tickler file under the date when payment is expected. Each day this tickler file is reviewed, and follow-up activity is conducted on insurance that is tardy that day.

For instance, on April 5 the financial secretary reviews her insurance tickler file and sees that there are 12 insurance claim forms that were filed March 5. Those claims are pulled, and the patients' accounts are reviewed to determine if the claims have been paid. Those that have not been paid are included in the financial secretary's workload for telephone follow-up that day. Note here that I said *telephone follow-up*. At this stage do not send duplicate claims under the assumption that the previously filed claim has been "lost in the mail." Do not do follow-up by writing letters to insurance companies or to your patients at this time. Just as when trying to collect from a delinquent patient, collection activity with a delinquent insurance company is most effective when done by telephone.

The purpose for follow-up on delinquent insurance is not to try to get the insurance companies to pay any sooner. You would rarely, if ever, be successful in obtaining that result. The purpose for conducting insurance follow-up is to determine the reason why the claim has not been paid and to make that determination as early as possible. Invariably when reviewing insurance in client offices I find patient delinquency related directly to tardy insurance claims. I often find the insurance was filed 45, 60, or even 90 days earlier. Ultimately a call is made to the insurance company only to find that the claim form never arrived, or the claim was incomplete and was sent to the patient for completion, or the claim was paid but the money was sent to the patient, or the claim was paid to the doctor's office but perhaps applied to the wrong account. The purpose for follow-up with insurance companies is to find out at the earliest possible date if this type of problem exists and to find out 30 days from the date the claim was filed rather than 60 or 90 days.

If the staff member makes a phone call to the insurance company and finds out that the claim is scheduled to be paid in a few days, she would take the insurance document and place it in the corresponding date in the 1-31 follow-up file. As claims are paid, this follow-up document will be removed from the 1–31 system.

The key to any type of 1–31 tickler file is that a commitment be made to using this system on a daily basis. Any 1–31 system will quickly fall apart if this commitment to daily activity does not exist.

Some Additional Questions and Answers About Insurance

"Tell me again why we should accept assignment of insurance benefits."

The answer is to better serve your patients. The more cared for your patients feel, the better their relationship will be with your practice. With that will come more case acceptance, better referrals, and more cooperative patients. Yes, accepting assignment of benefits takes more time; yes, it means dealing with problems related to insurance filing; yes, it means more paperwork; yes, it means more expense. And all of that — time, work, and expense — is insignificant when compared with the benefits associated with accepting assignment of insurance.

"Why shouldn't I pre-authorize my insurance claims? I find it impossible to accurately estimate insurance benefits, and my patients always ask me to pre-authorize."

The answer to this question is simple; 35–50% of patients on whom you do pre-authorizations will never come back to have the diagnosed work completed. Are you really willing to lose that high a percentage of your patients? As previously mentioned, with effort and commitment by the financial secretary, insurance can be estimated accurately.

"What happens when the insurance doesn't pay as much as I estimated?"

When you deal with quality patients and clearly inform them that 1) your estimate of insurance benefits is exactly that, an estimate, and 2) if the insurance company should pay any less they will be liable for the difference, then you should not have any problems in collecting.

"What if I need to present a treatment plan and financial arrangement to a patient but I am unable to estimate insurance coverage right now?"

If you have no information on that particular employer's insurance plan, and it is impossible to obtain this information by telephone, then you have two choices: 1) make a financial arrangement anyway making an educated estimate of potential insurance coverage (allowing for deductibles, etc.), or 2) advise the patient that you will contact the insurance company, get the insurance estimated, and handle the financial arrangement by phone (and, of course, schedule the patient for the recommended treatment if you can).

"What do I do when no matter how much work I do on the phone the insurance company absolutely will not help me in estimating insurance coverage?"

There are a number of ways of dealing with this:

1. Call the employer's personnel office and ask them to help with the information.

2. Review the employee's health benefits booklet.

3. Review the EOB's (Explanation of Benefits from the benefit checks of previous patients who work at the same employer).

4. Guess. This is not as crazy as it may seem. Tell your patient in advance that you are unable to get definitive information and that you are making an educated guess, which may be way off. If your patient will accept treatment and make a financial arrangement based on your educated guess, you have done a great job. Make sure your patient understands that if your guess is off he will be liable for any difference.

5. Pre-estimate. No, this is not a contradiction to everything I have previously said. Pre-estimates are, in general, inappropriate and should never be done *except* when there is absolutely no other way to determine insurance coverage, *and* the patient will not accept your diagnosis and schedule an appointment without definitive insurance information.

"Why can't I send a letter to the insurance company when doing follow-up instead of calling?"

For the same reason that you should rarely have a collection letter be your first choice as a method of dealing with a delinquent patient. Generally speaking, telephone activity is more productive than activity conducted by letter. Your own experience shows that rarely do insurance companies respond to follow-up letters. Remember the purpose for insurance follow-up is to determine *now* what the status of a particular insurance claim is. Seventy-five to 85% of the time, with one two-to-four-minute phone call, you can determine whether a claim has been denied, is pending, has already been paid, or has been sent for review. With a letter to an insurance company, you know nothing for weeks, and that is assuming they do respond.

Superbills

Many offices are not computerized, and filing a number of insurance forms on a daily basis is more time-consuming than it is for the computerized office. I suggest that these "manual" offices use a "Superbill" (Fig. 11–3). A Superbill properly used can dramatically reduce the workload of the administrative staff while at the same time improving counter collections.

You will note that the upper half of a Superbill looks like a standard ADA insurance claim form. It has patient information and insured information, along with employer and related information. It includes an assignment of benefits along with an authorization to release information. The lower half of the form is custom designed for each individual dental office. You will note in the sample form there are certain procedures listed by ADA code number and by name of procedure. This section of the form is individually designed by each office. The dental procedures the office does most often are identified and preprinted on the bottom half of the Superbill. Notice also that there are a number of blank spaces where less frequently performed procedures can be identified. This form is normally printed on NCR paper in triplicate and is most often used as follows:

The top half of the form is completed by the patient or an administrative staff person upon the patient's arrival in the office. The document goes with the patient into the operatory. Then the chairside or hygienist indicates on the form which procedure was done *and the fee for that procedure*. The document is given to the patient when he is dismissed from the operatory with instructions to return the document to the receptionist. The receptionist accepts this document and uses it as a tool to conduct her financial discussion as follows: "Mrs. Smith, your charges are $120. Your insurance should cover approximately $80 of that. If you would like to take care of your share of $40 today, we can offer you a 5% discount." The patient either pays or does not pay, and without regard to the results of the financial discussion, the third copy of the Superbill is separated from the first two and is presented to the patient. In this manner, each patient has an itemized list of the treatment done for the day and the fee for that treatment. The receptionist would have checked, of course, to ensure that the patient has signed the Superbill in the indicated areas.

The original of this document is then folded and immediately mailed to the insurance company. There is nothing more to fill out since the top half was

PLEASE RETURN THIS FORM TO THE RECEPTIONIST

ATTENDING DENTIST'S STATEMENT
☐ PAYMENT
☐ PRE-TREATMENT ESTIMATE

1. Patient Name
2. Relationship to Employee: Self | Spouse | Child | Other
3. Sex: M | F
4. Patient Birthdate: Mo. | Day | Year
5. If Full Time Student: School | City

6. Employee/Subscriber Name: First | Middle | Last
7. Employee/Subscriber Social Security No.
9. Name of Group Dental Program

8. Employee/Subscriber Mailing Address
City, State, Zip
10. Employer (Company) Name and Address

11. Group Number
12. Location (Local)
13. Are Other Family Members Employed? Employee Name | Soc. Sec. No.
14. Name and Address of Employer in Item 13

15. Is Patient Covered By Another Dental Plan? | Dental Plan Name | Union Local | Group No. | Name and Address of Carrier

RELEASE I authorize the doctor or insurance company to release any information required for payment of review of this claim. I am financially responsible for any balance due. I authorize my insurance benefits be paid directly to the undersigned dentist.

PATIENT SIGNATURE

X-RAYS: Enclosed Yes ( ) No ( ) Number
PROSTHETICS: Initial Placement: Yes ( ) No
If no, reason for replacement
Date of Prior Placement ____________________
I hereby certify that the procedures dated below have been completed.

Doctor Signature

Tooth # or Letter	Surface	DESCRIPTION OF SERVICES	Date Service Performed Mo Day Yr	ADA NO.	FEE	For Admin. Use Only
		DIAGNOSTIC				
		Initial Exam		00110		
		Periodic Exam		00120		
		Emergency Exam		00130		
		Single First Film		00220		
		Each Add'l. Film		00230		
		2 Bitewing Films		00272		
		4 Bitewing Films		00274		
		Panoramic Film		00330		
		Photographs		00471		
		Study Models		00470		
		PREVENTIVE				
		Adult Prophy		01110		
		Child Prophy		01120		
		Prophy-Fluoride		01201		
		Perio Scale/FM		04340		
		Perio Scale/Quad.		04341		
		Rt. Plane/Curr		04220		
		RESTORATIVE				
		Amalgam		02		
		Amalgam		02		
		Amalgam		02		
		Amalgam		02		
		Amalgam		02		
		Pin Retention		02190		
		Composite		023		
		Composite		023		
		Composite		023		
		ENDODONTICS				
		Root Canal		033		
		Pulp		03		
		Post & Core		02892		

Tooth # or Letter	Surface	DESCRIPTION OF SERVICES	Date Service Performed Mo Day Yr	ADA NO.	FEE	For Admin. Use Only
		CROWN & BRIDGE				
		Porcelain to Gold		02750		
		Full Gold		02790		
		S. S. Crown		02830		
		PFG Abutment		06750		
		FG Abutment		06790		
		Pontic PFG		06240		
		Pontic FG		06210		
		ORAL SURGERY				
		Extraction, Simple		07110		
		Extraction, Add'l.		07120		
		Surgical		07		
		PROSTHETICS				
		Full Denture U-L		05		
		Partial Denture U-L		05		
		Reline U-L		05		
		OTHER				

TOTAL FEE CHARGED	
MAX. ALLOWABLE	
DEDUCTIBLE	
CARRIER %	
CARRIER PAYS	
PATIENT PAYS	

Fig. 11–3

filled out prior to the patient being seen by the doctor or hygienist, and the bottom half was filled out by the clinical employee. Utilization of a Superbill in this manner will ensure that insurance is billed on a daily basis for all work that has been done on that day. The second copy of the Superbill is used for your insurance follow-up documentation.

Many doctors request that patients bring their own insurance forms when they come for treatment. This works most of the time. However, many times patients forget to bring their forms and the result is delayed insurance billing. The Superbill will help to solve this problem.

There is another advantage in the use of this form as described. In some situations, patients — especially delinquent patients — will by-pass the front desk because they are in a hurry or because they don't want to make a financial arrangement or have any other kind of conversation about money. If the patient has been instructed in the operatory to hand a document to the receptionist, this ensures that each patient has had a financial discussion prior to leaving the office.

Some people say, "Insurance companies in our area do not accept this type of claim." This is simply not true. A properly designed Superbill such as the one included in Figure 11–3 is accepted by every insurance company in the United States with the exception of closed-panel (participating) companies. I described this type of company earlier in this chapter. You *may* find that some self-insured employers will not accept Superbills as well. But since in most areas of the country, self-insured employers make up a very small minority of all claims filed, this should not be a problem. Many closed-panel companies (notably Delta, Blue Cross, and Blue Shield) will not accept a Superbill such as the one I have included. However, all three of these organizations will accept Superbills if they are designed to meet their particular requirements. Please check with your local companies for proper design requirements.

Summary

Although filing insurance may be a pain in the neck, it will enhance the well-being of the fee-for-service private practice dental office. Filing insurance on your patient's behalf, accepting assignment of insurance benefits, and handling routine insurance-related problems from your office on your patients' behalf will go far to improve the relationship between the patients and your practice. And improving that relationship is what this book is all about.

CHAPTER 12

RECEIVABLES MANAGEMENT (COMMONLY KNOWN AS COLLECTION ACTIVITY AND DELINQUENCY CONTROL)

The first part of this book was intended to introduce you to a philosophy of patient management. When the recommendations flowing from that philosophy are implemented, you will eventually surround yourself with patients of impeccable quality. Included with that impeccable quality will be patients with a high degree of stability and integrity. The bottom line for patients with integrity (your "A" patients) is that they will keep the agreements that they make.

Except when they don't! I am a person of integrity and you are a person of integrity. Yet, we have both failed to keep agreements from time to time. Circumstances or "things" happen to us in our lives. These circumstances may make it difficult or impossible to keep an agreement. The same is true even with your best "A" patients. I am sure you have some "A" patients who have such a high regard for you and the services you have provided that they would pay your debt before all others. You can, therefore, count on being appropriately paid by them even during times of financial hardship.

There are other patients (who are also "A" patients) who will pay you perfectly as long as things go well for them. However, when they hit a glitch in life, that glitch may cause delinquency in your practice. Does that mean this is not an "A" patient and that you should kick that patient out of your practice? Of course not.

Receivables Management: Its Purpose

Before going further, I want to state the purpose of collection activity, and, more important, what is *not* the purpose of collection activity. One of the most important things for the financial secretary to remember is that the purpose of collection activity is *not* to collect a payment. Before you write me off as a maniac and burn this book, let me explain. *The primary purpose for collection activity is problem resolution.* Yes, certainly, the problem is that the account is past due. But a larger and more significant problem caused by delinquency is one of relationship.

If a patient is delinquent in paying his account and has failed to keep his agreement, he has created a negative relationship with the practice. When your patient is in a negative relationship with the practice, he is less likely to contribute to your well-being and more likely to contribute in a negative manner. This has been discussed earlier in this book. Take a look at who is not accepting your diagnosis. Who is being clinically uncooperative? Who is missing appointments? Who shows up late for appointments? Who complains about the quality of your care? And take a close look at who files malpractice suits. You will find that 70% or more of all of these problems come from patients whose accounts are delinquent. After experiencing the larger problems generated by delinquency, I would think the problem of a patient being $100 past due would pale in comparison.

Delinquency control and collection activity have been looked upon as negative activity. The "collector" was often viewed by the doctor, staff, and patients as the "bad guy." Any financial secretary who considers her primary obligation to be collecting payments from delinquent patients has, no doubt, found herself in this position.

In addition, many doctors view collection activity as uncomfortable for the patient. These offices feared that such activity might cause the patient to become alienated from the practice. Doctors also feared patients would no longer refer to the practice and might even leave the practice. Because of these fears, collection activity was postponed for periods of time or left undone.

I often find that our new clients fail to send monthly statements to every patient. These offices consider statements as "bills." Therefore, they send them to delinquent patients only. As a symbol of delinquency, the statement becomes a threat to the patient and is looked upon as negative. Such offices send statements to patients after they become 30 days delinquent. Typically, no collection activity is conducted for another 30 days. Then another statement is sent out. Quite often this statement contains a handwritten note, a Day Glo sticker, or a rubber stamped message indicating that the account is "Past Due." Such offices also make no attempt (at least not at this level of delinquency) to communicate directly with the patient either by telephone or by letter to determine if the patient had a problem with paying his bill or if the office could be of some assistance in resolving any problem.

Recall the earlier example where I demonstrated the decline in moral obligation of a patient as his debt becomes more and more delinquent. Very often the lack of appropriate collection activity, which was an effort not to alienate the patient, turns out to be exactly the cause of the patient's alienation. A vicious circle is established which perpetuates the delinquency problem.

Receivables Management: An Example

Many years ago in the banking and consumer finance industry, I discovered that the "righteous" employees interested only in getting moneys due had a much worse collection percentage than those employees who were sincerely interested in assisting their customers in resolving the problem. The problem was, of course, that the account was past due. The finance industry learned that if they could keep their debtors current, those debtors would continue to be quality, contributing members of that financial institution and they would refer other quality clients. Think for a moment what would happen if you had an account with GMAC, Ford Motor Credit, or Chrysler Credit and you became delinquent and ultimately one of those organizations had to repossess your car? Would you ever be able to finance a car at that organization again? Of course not. You lose in that situation. But so, also, does the financing institution. Banks, finance companies, credit unions, and retail stores offering charge accounts would not long survive without their credit business. They learned long ago to contact their customers quickly once an account became past due, their intention being to resolve the delinquency, resolve the relationship, and keep that customer or client purchasing more product, borrowing more money, or buying more cars.

By studying the credit and collection policies of any major financial institution in this country, you can see the folly in the way collection activity has typically been done in the health care business. If your intention is to maintain quality relationships with your patients, then a patient who becomes delinquent must be contacted immediately. But the focus of that contact is problem resolution, not collections.

Suppose Mr. Smith has a current account balance of $400. He has a financial arrangement with you for $100 a month. He has made no payments in the past two months and is, therefore, $200 past due. A phone call is made to the patient, and the patient promises to send you $100 in the mail immediately. Two days later, sure enough, the $100 has arrived in your practice as promised. Was that a good collection call? I certainly don't think so. You still have a patient who is $100 past due. You do not know what caused the delinquency. You do not know how or if the continuing delinquency is going to be resolved. There has been little or no improvement in the relationship. And it is extremely likely that the relationship has deteriorated further. Collecting that $100 may very well have damaged the practice much more than it helped.

But let's go back to my earlier statement: The purpose of collection activity is problem resolution. The problem is not the delinquency so much as it is the patient in a negative relationship with the practice. While that patient is in a negative relationship, he will not or cannot contribute to your well-being. This causes true damage to the practice. The goal of collection activity is to restore that patient relationship to positive ground. But just as in the old adage "there is more than one way to skin a cat," so also is there more than one way to accomplish this objective.

How to Return the Patient Relationship to Positive Ground

One way is to collect the account in full. That method of problem resolution should be considered in every collection contact you make.

A second method is to collect all of the delinquent portion of the account and have the patient recommit to keeping his financial agreement with the practice in the future.

But there are other acceptable solutions to the problem. What if as a result of your collection call you determine that the patient is not capable of making up his past-due payments? Perhaps your patient was laid off work for three weeks, during which time he had no income. Now that he is back at work, he can make his promised payments each month; however, he does not have the means to make up his past-due payments. In such a situation it would be appropriate to add his delinquent payments to the end of his financial agreement. This would extend his agreement for a month or more, but now you have helped the patient out of a bind. This result achieves the objective of restoring the patient relationship to positive ground.

An innovative and creative financial secretary who understands the true purpose of collection activity will be willing and ready to work with a cooperative patient to bring that patient back into a quality, mutually nurturing relationship with the practice. This may involve extending the contract as in the previous example. It may involve increasing the monthly payments to catch up some delinquency. It may involve allowing the patient to skip a month to help him through a bind. Any solution should be sought as long as it is reasonable. (Sorry, six months without payments is not reasonable and neither is $10 a month.) Remember that once a new agreement has been made, the old agreement ceases to exist and the patient *is no longer delinquent.*

Also, recall the financial secretary in my friend's office who had to dismiss my sister from the practice. The financial secretary did a magnificent job of problem resolution and yet she did not collect a cent. The problem in that instance was the practice had a delinquent patient in a negative relationship with the practice. The resolution of the problem was dismissal of the patient. Upon that dismissal they no longer had a delinquent patient in a negative relationship. The patient was no longer delinquent because the account was written off as uncollectible. The patient was not in a negative relationship, because the patient had been dismissed.

It is important to recognize no matter how committed your practice has been to credit management and accounts receivable control, no matter how well you have investigated your patients and reviewed patient history forms and obtained credit reports, no matter how promptly or efficiently you have conducted collection activity, you may still make mistakes. You will have a patient you are unable to keep in a quality relationship, and it will become necessary to dismiss him from the practice. That is an acceptable end result to collection activity. There is not a business of any type in this country today (including the health care community) that grants credit without sustaining loss from time to time. If discontinuation of a patient and writing off an account balance is looked upon as failure, you will be forever unwilling to take that step.

Summary

The purpose of collection activity is problem resolution, and the intended result of collection activity is to re-establish and maintain a high quality relationship with your patients. Once you have changed the emphasis of collection activity from collecting money to re-establishing relationship, delinquency control activity will then be looked upon as a very positive practice-building activity.

CHAPTER 13

DELINQUENCY FOLLOW-UP

In order for collection activity to be effective, it must be consistent—conducted daily. It also must be credible. Your patients must understand that if they make an agreement with you and fail to keep it, they will be held accountable. While most health care practices accept this philosophy, rarely is it put into practice. In order to have a collection system that obtains the results you want, you must:

1. Identify which patients are past due.
2. Follow up on those delinquent patients promptly and consistently enough to resolve the problem.

The Typical Follow-up Scenario

The typical health care practice is fairly good about contacting (conducting collection activity on) delinquent patients. These contacts usually yield a promise to bring the account up to date or to make a specific payment by a specific time period—by the 10th of the month. Then the 10th of the month comes and goes and the promised payment does not arrive in the practice. Often there is no further contact with that patient for a week or perhaps even a month following that missed payment. The patient, therefore, gets a mixed message. On the one hand, the first contact indicates the practice desires to be paid for the treatment provided. On the other hand, a broken promise and no follow-up within a reasonable time period tells the patient that the practice is not too concerned about the debt. This inconsistency does nothing to solve the delinquency problem and, in fact, creates a bigger problem. Patients conclude that it is acceptable to miss their payments and not keep the agreements they have made.

As a result of this inconsistency, patients become more and more delinquent, causing a further deterioration in the relationship with the practice. These delinquency problems will inevitably create new problems in the area of no-shows, cancellations, non-acceptance of diagnosis, poor referral rates, and other problems which I have mentioned previously.

Once we recognize the need to conduct collection activity promptly, there must be a method in the office that allows the financial secretary to identify which patients need collection activity on which particular day. There are dozens of systems available, but the most basic, and the one that always works is a 1–31 card file.

The 1–31 Follow-up System

When the financial secretary is comfortable with the use of the 1–31 system in its basic form, she can use her imagination to come up with many ways its effectiveness can be enhanced.

Once a patient has been identified as past due, either by review of an aged receivables report, delinquency report, or by scanning the ledger cards for new delinquency (this scan of cards or review of computer reports should be done on a weekly basis), a decision is made whether telephone collection activity or letter collection is appropriate. Then the first collection call is made or the first collection letter is written. Next, the patient's name is placed on an index card along with the date a response is due and, perhaps, the details of that patient's financial agreement with the practice.

If a patient's account is 10 days past due, some form of collection activity needs to be conducted. Let's say that Ed Smith's payment was due on June 1. On June 10 the payment is identified as being 10 days late. At this point the financial secretary determines the most effective collection activity is a preprinted late notice and this is mailed to the patient. An index card is made for Mr. Smith and the date the late notice was sent is noted. Assume the financial secretary intends to follow up on this account, if she has not received a payment or appropriate response, within 10 days. Therefore, Mr. Smith's index card is placed in a file separated by 31 dividers, one for each day of the month. Since she wants to conduct follow-up 10 days from the date the late notice was sent (June 10), Mr. Smith's follow-up card is placed behind the 20th.

With another patient the financial secretary may decide to make a phone call. She calls Mrs. Jones, who promises to have a payment into office by the 13th. A follow-up card is made for Mrs. Jones and placed in the 1–31 file behind the 13th.

This process is followed with every collection phone call and every collection letter. With each type of collection activity, a date for appropriate follow-up is determined and a follow-up card is placed in the 1–31 follow-up file after that date.

Each day the financial secretary reviews her 1–31 file and removes the cards that were placed behind the previous day's date. For instance, on the 21st of the month she would pull all the follow-up cards that were placed behind the 20th. Those represent every patient who promised to have a payment into the office by the 20th. She reviews those cards and checks them against the patient's account. If the promised payment has been made, the index card is replaced in the 1–31 file under a date that allows for an appropriate grace period before the financial secretary intends to conduct further collection activity. For instance, if Mr. Smith's regular monthly payment is due on the first, she would probably place his follow-up card behind the 10th, thereby allowing a 10 day grace period.

In reviewing the index cards on a daily basis, the financial secretary will find accounts that have not paid according to the agreement. Consequently, further collection activity can be conducted literally the same day or the day following the date that a payment was due or promised.

Offices that use computerized accounting systems should use these index cards to document not only the terms of a patient's financial agreement, but also the details of the collection activity that has been conducted. This index card serves as a permanent record of that patient's activity in the practice.

An example of the power of this type of documentation follows:

Financial secretary: "Mrs. Jones, I spoke with your husband at work on the 17th of last month. He promised to have a $65 payment in our office by today."

This communication, based on your documentation of past collection activity, is much more effective than:

Financial secretary: "Mrs. Jones, I am calling about your past due account."

In addition, by documenting collection activity in such a manner, a financial secretary can identify by reviewing past activity what has and has not worked. Perhaps letters got no results but phone calls collected payments. Or, every time she reached the husband, she received a promise that was ultimately not kept. Every time she reached the wife, she received a promise that was kept. Clearly this information would increase the effectiveness of any future collection activity. As you can see, thorough documentation is an imperative part of any 1–31 follow-up system.

The 1–31 Pitfall

Unfortunately, the 1–31 system fails from time to time. The problem is usually temporary; nevertheless, the failure causes severe problems with respect to lost cash flow and diminished relationship with patients. Whenever the system fails, it always fails for the same reason: lack of commitment to utilize the system daily.

You can see from reviewing this method, that on Monday it will be necessary for the financial secretary to review three days' cards: Friday, Saturday, and Sunday. This means the amount of collection activity to be conducted on Monday is far greater than on Friday. If, in addition, the financial secretary was home sick on Monday, then on Tuesday there are four days to pull. You can see how failure could quickly result if there was not a real commitment to working the system every workday. It all goes back to what was said in an earlier chapter: the priority for conducting collection activity needs to be as strong as the priority for providing care or answering your telephone.

Summary

To be successful, collection activity must be conducted promptly and consistently. In addition, collection activity must educate patients that failure to keep payment agreements is not acceptable and they will be held accountable.

The 1–31 system just described is one of the most efficient and effective methods of achieving prompt, consistent collection activity. This system allows for easy follow up and ample documentation. Installing it is simple and requires little expense. Once the financial secretary has become comfortable with the system in its basic form, it can be easily modified or enhanced to meet personal preferences or reflect innovative ideas.

I highly recommend the 1–31 system. However, as long as a practice commits to using a follow-up system on a consistent day-to-day basis, I encourage use of any system which suits the person using it.

Follow-up systems are an integral part of successful collection activity. Therefore, if you are committed to the highest possible quality of life within your practice, you must find a system that works for you and use it.

CHAPTER 14

COLLECTION ACTIVITY METHODS: PART I

Your success at fulfilling the purpose of Receivables Management (Collection Activity) depends on the collection methods or techniques you employ. In my experience there are only three effective collection activity methods. They are 1) face-to-face contact with a patient before or after an appointment, 2) telephone calls, and 3) letters.

I have been in hundreds of offices and invariably these offices choose one of the above three methods as their primary means of collection activity. Some offices talk with delinquent patients before or after an appointment. Others, believing that method is too confrontive, strictly make telephone calls. And others, believing even telephone calls are confrontive, prefer the more anonymous collection letter.

Used alone, each of these three methods is somewhat effective. However, I believe the best way to conduct collection activity is to use these three methods in balance.

Collection Activity: Conduct it Promptly and Consistently

The most important thing to remember about collection activity is this: conduct it immediately. I am writing this chapter just after visiting a new client's office whose policy was to send a statement only after the patient was 55 days past due. This office had enormous delinquency. Yet, they failed to realize that this collection activity method, coupled with their reluctance to use more effective methods, was creating the problem they sought to avoid. They were training their patients to believe it was acceptable to become 55 days delinquent. They reinforced this belief further by taking no other action until another statement was sent 30 days later. In many cases, a patient three months delinquent becomes a severe collection problem.

To be effective, collection activity must be consistent. This means collection activity must be conducted each day the financial secretary is in the office.

Certainly, by conducting collection activity sporadically, by using only one or two of the three available methods of collection activity, and by starting collection activity only after accounts are 30 or more days late, delinquency can be maintained at a certain level of control. However, if your commitment is to eliminate delinquency as a negative issue for the practice and bring your delinquent accounts under total and absolute control, conducting collection activity must be a priority equal to scheduling appointments, answering the phone, and diagnosing care. Just as you would never dream of allowing a phone to ring unanswered, a practice committed to credit management and accounts receivable control would never allow a day to go by without appropriate collection activity. In addition, no avenue or method of collection activity would go unexplored.

Collection Activity: The Key to Success

The difference between an office that is truly successful in conducting collection activity and one that has mediocre success is "the place the practice comes from." By this statement I mean there is a sound basis or reason for your office conducting the collection activity. That reason is not to collect the past-due account but, as stated earlier, is to resolve a relationship problem with the patient. With that as your ultimate purpose and goal along with a true commitment by the practice to dedicate the time and tools necessary to resolve the problem, delinquency in the practice can become a thing of the past in as little as six months. That is certainly a worthy and realistic goal.

There are three primary means of collection activity. One is face-to-face communication with a patient. Ultimately this is the most effective means of collection activity. However, collection activity should begin prior to the work being done and prior to a debt being incurred. Essentially, a clearly documented financial arrangement made at the time treatment is diagnosed and prior to the time work is provided will reduce the need for collection activity. Establish financial arrangement parameters that meet the patient's level of stability and credit worthiness. One only has to review existing accounts to see the significant delinquency caused primarily because sound financial arrangements were not made prior to the time treatment was diagnosed. No matter how careful your staff is in their credit evaluation, and no matter how efficiently your treatment presentations and financial arrangements are managed, even the best "A+" patients may become delinquent. It is at this point that the following two methods of collection activity — telephone calls and letters — come into play. I'll discuss telephone collection activity first.

Telephone Collection Activities

Years of conducting and analyzing collection activity by various banks, finance companies, and health care practices around the country has shown that telephone collection is, without a doubt, the most efficient and effective means of collection activity available to the health care practice. By using the telephone you are assured that your communication gets to the party responsible for payment. You have no such assurance with letters. With telephone collection you can make specific verbal requests of the patient. You have an opportunity to obtain a response, negotiate with the patient, and be empathetic and considerate of the patient's needs. More important, you can make certain the patient understands your empathy and consideration. At the same time, you can explain your position to the patient. This allows for an interaction that you intend to result in a mutually agreeable decision on how this delinquency problem will be resolved.

Many years ago, the Bell Telephone System conducted research on telephone collection policies and procedures. Over a period of time, they developed a method of telephone collection that was immediately identified as highly effective. To this day, I have never found another system which surpasses it in efficiency and consistency of result. The premise of this system is the same as the premise you have read in previous paragraphs in this book: Problem resolution through effective communication with your patients.

Operating from this premise, Bell Telephone Systems devised a two-stage plan for making an effective collection telephone call. The description of the plan is directed to your financial secretary or the person in the practice who actually does the collection activity. If she is an "old hand" at collection activity, she will recognize these two stages, and the steps within the stages are nothing more than the natural progression of a collection call. Nevertheless, perhaps reviewing these steps will help remind her of some of the key procedures she may not remember due to the day-to-day pressures of her job. If she is new at collection activity, becoming familiar with these steps will give her solid direction.

Stage One: Pre-call Planning

The first stage in collection starts with pre-call planning— what you do before you even make a phone call. Perhaps a patient's account is two to three weeks overdue. Your first impulse may be to call and demand payment. If you are not well prepared, you could end up with poor results. On the other hand, if you are well prepared — you know the available facts and have them in front of you — you can discuss the account on the basis of those facts. Odds are you will not get caught off guard and your collection efforts will pay off (no pun intended).

In order to know the facts and have them available to you, you must conduct pre-call planning as the first step in making a really effective collection call. To conduct pre-call planning, follow these seven steps:

1. Find out if the practice is at fault — no statement sent, account not updated with last payment, posting error, etc.
2. Find out what previous collection efforts have been taken and the results.
3. Find out the patient's past payment record.
4. Find out who the responsible party is.
5. Predetermine a potential payment plan.

6. Prepare fact-finding questions.
7. Prepare an opening statement.

Let's take a look at these seven steps in more detail.

Step 1. Find out if the practice is at fault. Check all of your records on this patient's account for payments received and not noted. Did the patient actually receive *all* of the care that has been put on the books? Is your ledger correct? Did the patient have a complaint that has not been settled? Is there a problem with insurance that has not been adequately handled? If the answer to any of these questions is "yes," take immediate action to resolve the problem(s). Do your best to resolve them prior to making the collection phone call. If the answer to these questions is "no," chances are the practice is not at fault, and the late payment is just that—late.

Step 2. Find out what previous collection steps have been taken, if any, and when. This means two things. First, determine what collection measures have been taken on the payment that is overdue now. In addition, review measures taken at other times the account has been overdue. Were collection letters sent? Were phone calls made? Has there been personal contact while the patient was in the office? Second, find out what the results were.

Very often the financial secretary of a practice depends on memory to document previous collection activity. This is usually inadequate. If documentation is available, the person making the collection call can quickly determine who has been spoken to in the past, what the basics of that conversation were, and what previous promises have been made. The more she knows about the practice's past dealings with that patient, the better she can conduct each successive collection phone call.

Step 3. Find out the patient's past payment record. How often has this account been overdue in the past? Is there a pattern? For example, is this patient overdue every month? Every other month? In the summer? Around holidays? Evaluate patterns you find, and decide if the patient is likely to pay or if the payment record will get worse.

For instance, patient Tom Smith's payment record indicates that he usually pays, but his payments come in only after a series of collection letters or a combination of letters and phone calls. In reviewing his account you notice he is up to his old tricks again. His account is overdue. How would being aware of Tom's past history change the way you deal with him on the phone this time?

How about patient Donald Brown? He signed a financial agreement with you several months ago. The first month's payment was about two weeks late. The second month's payment was three weeks late. Every time Donald was called, he was always polite, always happy to pay. His fifth payment came in four weeks late, and only after another phone call. What do you think will ultimately happen with Donald's account if this history is allowed to continue?

Step 4. Find out who the responsible party is. Only the person legally responsible for paying the bill is the right person to talk with—not a secretary, a partner, a child, a mother-in-law, a neighbor, an ex-wife, or an ex-husband. Here again is where good records pay off. Trying to collect from anyone else would be a waste of your time and could be embarrassing to both you and your patient. Depending on your disclosure of specifics, talking to the wrong person could become a legal problem. Remember, a well-designed patient history form and good record documentation will give you the information you need in this area.

Step 5. The heart of your collection effort is to predetermine a potential payment plan. A sound payment plan is a schedule of specific amounts to be paid at specific times that keeps the account balance up-to-date and paid in full within a specific time. Therefore, the payment plan cannot be arbitrary. On one hand, it has to call for amounts and dates acceptable to the patient and within his ability to pay. By the same token, the practice has to accept this payment plan also. The amounts and the time schedule have to be realistic as far as the practice is concerned. In this regard, the practice policies will tell you just how flexible you can be.

It is important that I restate that the payment must be acceptable to the patient. Please note I did not say "comfortable." Very often financial secretaries believe they have an obligation to make a financial agreement that is comfortable for patients. But all too often such payment is entirely unrealistic and uncomfortable for you.

Without a specific payment plan, the collection call could simply be harassment—an attempt to collect all that is due without regard to the patient's circumstances or other facts that may surround the overdue account.

Getting a person to agree to a payment plan is really selling them on it. As in any form of selling, the goal is to help the person see some benefit in buying whatever it is you are selling. In short, any time that you ask someone to buy something, one of the first questions they ask themselves is, "What's in it for me?" In the case of an overdue account, you are asking the patient to buy "your payment plan" to bring his account up to date or to pay it off. But why should he? What's in it for him? What are some of the benefits of bringing his account up to date?

A Good Payment Plan: Patient Benefits

Historically, in the health care field, there were very few direct or indirect benefits for keeping an account current. Conversely, there were very few penalties to patients for allowing their accounts to become seriously delinquent. Typically, the practice continued to provide health care and conducted little or no collection activity.

There are two benefits patients receive for keeping their account current: 1) protection of credit ratings and 2) assurance of continuing health care from your practice. To make these benefits real for your patients, I recommend reporting any patient's negative credit to your local credit bureau. It will then go on your patient's permanent credit record. In addition, I recommend denying or limiting continued dental care in appropriate cases. Besides the few that I have just mentioned, can you think of other benefits a patient might gain by bringing his account up to date?

Once again, the definition of a sound payment plan is a schedule of specific amounts to be paid at specific times so the overdue account will be up to date within a reasonable but specific time.

Step 6. Prepare fact-finding questions. The purpose of asking fact-finding questions is to help you find out why the patient is not paying his bill on time. In addition, such questions help you decide if the payment plan you have worked out is practical. Do the facts you uncover lead you to believe that the patient is able to pay according to the plan you have worked out? A good fact-finding question is searching, open-ended, and requires the other person to answer in detail rather than with "yes" or "no." Open-ended questions begin with "who," "what," "when," "where," "why," or "how." For example, "What's happened in the last month or two, Mrs. Brown, that caused your account to become past due? Perhaps I can help." Remember, good fact-finding questions also help you find out if your payment plan is practical. Once you decide the plan is practical, proceed to sell your patient on it. If you decide it is not practical, adjust the plan as necessary, and then sell the patient on it. Remember, fact-finding questions are open-ended and should bring out the reason for the non-payment.

Step 7. Prepare an opening statement. This step has three parts: 1) identify yourself and the doctor for whom you work, 2) give the specific reason for your phone call, and 3) make a strategic pause. The first 15 to 20 seconds of your collection call are the most important. Even though you are making a collection call, you must capture the person's willingness to listen. Your opening statement should be pleasant, confident, relaxed, and warm. It should not be cold or disinterested. By the same token, you cannot leave any doubt that you are calling about an overdue account. It is not easy, but deciding in advance how you are going to handle your opening statement will help.

I want to stress a point about the strategic pause. This pause is used to shift the burden of conversation to the patient and to get him/her to acknowledge the purpose of the call. Different responses will ensue: a simple acknowledgment, a full explanation of why the account is overdue, an apology, an offer to pay, or whatever. Many times, this simple step can make a collection call successful without going any further.

Always open with a statement, never a question. For example, "This is Lenora from Dr. Carter's office, and I note that we did not receive the $80 payment that was due on June 1." (Pause.) By stopping your conversation at that point the burden of conversation is placed squarely on the patient, which is your exact intention.

To this point I have been discussing the seven steps of pre-call planning. The primary concern of making the call in the first place is to make a successful collection effort. It is not enough to simply know the pre-call planning steps. You also have to know their sequence, and you have to use them in sequence. Again, in order:

1. Find out if the practice is at fault.
2. Find out what previous collection efforts have been taken and the results.
3. Find out the patient's past payment record.
4. Find out who the responsible party is.
5. Predetermine a potential payment plan.
6. Prepare fact-finding questions.
7. Prepare an opening statement. (Remember, there are three parts to that statement: identify yourself and your doctor, give the reason for the call, and make your strategic pause.)

Let me remind you that the success of the call could hinge on how well Step 7, the opening statement, is handled.

Making the Collection Call

Although pre-call planning is extremely important, the skill level of the person making the call most often determines its success. So let's get on to the steps of an actual call. First, there are eight key steps in making an effective collection call. The first three will sound quite familiar because they were prepared for in your pre-call planning:

1. Identify yourself and your doctor.
2. Give the reason for your phone call.
3. Make a strategic pause.
4. Ask fact-finding questions.
5. Create a bridge to the payment plan.
6. Present your payment plan.
7. Overcome objections.
8. Close the phone call.

Steps 1–3. The opening statement, of course, is a snap, or is it? People find it hard to stop talking once they get started. Yet that strategic pause could be the key to making the collection effort successful without going much further. It might get you an apology, an explanation, or an offer to pay. Perhaps all three. If the person on the other end of the line offers neither an explanation nor full payment, you would obviously go on to step 4.

Step 4. Ask fact-finding questions. Remember, you are going to present a payment plan to the patient that you have determined in your pre-call planning. However, you must be sensitive to the patient's situation and recognize that any payment plan you present must have credibility. It would be ineffective if you presented a payment plan when it was obvious the patient was in a situation that would make that payment plan untenable to him. The purpose of fact-finding questions is to determine the reason for the delinquency. Then, based on current facts, adjust the plan if necessary. As a result, the payment plan you present should be acceptable to the patient.

A fact-finding conversation might be, "What's happened in the past few months, Mrs. Malone, to cause you to fall behind in your payments?"

Mrs. Malone: "Actually, my husband was laid off work for two months and we couldn't get any unemployment. We fell way behind on our rent and practically everything else. It is going to take me four or five months to catch up."

Considering that the financial secretary had a predetermined payment plan to bring the account up to date within two months, what should she be doing at this point, at least in her mind?

Once you have the facts straight, once you understand the patient's situation and have made any adjustments to your proposed plan that you feel are necessary, go to Step 5.

Step 5. Create a bridge to the payment plan. Jumping into the details of the payment plan at this point and telling the patient how you want the account handled will probably get you poor results. To avoid this, make a transition to that payment plan with a bridging statement. This is where selling comes in. For instance, "From what you have just told me, Mrs. Malone, I think I have a plan that will make it easy for you to bring the account up to date and at least we can take that worry off your hands." The financial secretary offers two benefits in that statement: 1) she offered to make it easy for Mrs. Malone to bring the account up to date, and 2) she offered to take that worry off of her hands. One objective of the bridging statement is to let the patient know you are interested in helping her catch up, with the least amount of pain. Another objective is to presell the plan that you are about to present. Focus the patient's attention on the plan you intend to offer.

Another bridging statement might be, "Mrs. Malone, in reviewing what you have said to me, I think I have an idea that will help you bring your account current." The purpose of this statement is to make sure your patient understands that you have considered her response to your fact-finding questions and that you are compassionate and are aware of her needs.

Once you have made a bridging statement, go to Step 6.

Step 6. Present your payment plan. As I have mentioned, a sound payment plan includes a schedule of specific amounts to be paid at specific times so that the overdue account will be up to date within a reasonable time. What is reasonable? There are no hard and fast rules. It could be two, three, or four payments. With large treatment plans or ortho cases, it could be many more payments. It depends on the amount outstanding, what the patient is capable of paying and the office's internal financial policies. It may be the policy that an "A+" patient would be allowed to have payments as low as $50 a month over a period of 10 or 12 months. This type of payment plan may be productive and useful with "A+" patients, although it would undoubtedly be damaging if you were to use a policy like this for the "B" patients. And it would be ludicrous to have a payment plan like this for "C" patients.

Let's say you have called Mrs. Malone and introduced yourself. When you make your strategic pause, the patient says, "Look. I will send in my late payments very soon." Is that an acceptable payment plan? Does that include a schedule of specific amounts to be paid at specific times? The answer is NO. "Soon" isn't specific.

Let's review some other possible payment plans. After each one, you decide if it is a sound plan. What about, "Send in all of your late payments some time next month"? Certainly that is not a sound plan. It is not specific.

What about this one? "Send in payments of $100 on the 10th, the 15th, and the 20th of next month, and that will leave you with only a $100 balance left to pay." What do you think of that plan? It certainly is better than the first, but it still did not bring the account completely up to date. There is still a $100 balance for which there is no specific agreement.

What about this? "Send us $100 next Wednesday, another $100 on the 20th of the month, and the balance of $100 on the first of next month. Then continue with your regular monthly payments as per our previous agreement." Is that an appropriate payment plan? Yes, I certainly think so. It included specific amounts and specific dates, and it will bring the account fully up to date by the first of next month.

I want to point out here that the financial secretary has tremendous flexibility in determining payment plans. In the previous example, I showed a financial secretary proposing a very aggressive payment plan calling for a delinquent account to be paid up very quickly. This is just an example. Your financial secretary may or may not present payment plans such as this. Again, *it should depend on the patient's individual situation.* A financial secretary truly committed to resolving delinquency may decide to waive the delinquency, add the past-due amounts onto the end of the contract, and resolve the problem by extending the contract length. She may decide to have the patient increase monthly payment by $10 and catch up the delinquency that way. Any agreement that is reached, as long as it is realistic and acceptable to both parties, means that you have conducted a successful collection call.

Here's a short quiz. Are the following statements true or false?

1. More than one payment plan can be presented in a collection call. This is certainly true. Information gained during your fact-finding questions could cause you to change your original plan. As many payment plans as necessary can be presented to your patient to bring the account up to date. Of course, ultimately you have to settle on a single plan.

2. A payment plan is a schedule of payments designed to bring an overdue account up to date. That is true. That's the main purpose of the phone call.

3. Only the collector's plan should be considered. This is certainly false. Suppose the patient proposed a plan that would bring his account up to date or pay the account off sooner than you had originally planned. Or, perhaps the patient's plan, while not paying it off sooner than yours, is at least realistic and acceptable. Of course, you would accept the patient's suggestion if it is appropriate.

4. A payment plan should be specific in terms, amounts, and dates. True. Keep in mind that regardless of how many payments or how much each payment is or when they are paid, the basic purpose of your phone call is to get the patient to commit to a schedule of payments that make the account current by a specified time. Also recall that you have to sell a payment plan just as you have to sell any idea. The only way a patient will buy a plan is if he feels he will benefit by doing so. No matter how many benefits you offer, the first reaction to your initial payment plan may be an objection. That's the reason for Step 7.

Step 7. Overcoming objections. There are three parts to Step 7: 1) determine the patient's exact objection, 2) get agreement on the parts of the plan not objected to, and 3) work out an agreeable solution to the parts objected to. Generally speaking, most of the patient's objections are postponements—reasons for not agreeing to the payment plan you have proposed now. It is important that you understand the patient may not be objecting to all aspects of the payment plan you proposed.

For instance, Mr. Wilson's account has a $673 account balance. He has gone three months without a payment. You have proposed that he pay $300 by the 15th of this month, $200 by the 30th of the month, and the balance of $173 by the 10th of next month. His response, "I can't do that. Look, I'm in a real bind, and until my business picks up there is no way for me to pay according to that schedule."

No matter how you slice it, Mr. Wilson has made an objection. But it is a general objection, and you do not know if he is objecting to every aspect of your plan or just to one part of it. Consequently, the first thing you have to do at this point is to find out specifically what Mr. Wilson is objecting to. You ask and his answer is, "Like I said, there is no way for me to meet that payment schedule. In particular, not that $300 by the 15th of this month."

When you want someone to "buy" your payment plan, you have to "sell" someone on meeting it. When you are overcoming objections, the same rule applies. Let's review Mr. Wilson's objection again. " I can't do that. I'm in a real bind. Until my business picks up there is no way for me to meet that payment schedule."

You can then ask, "Just what part of that plan is difficult?" Mr. Wilson may reply, "Well, like I said, there is no way for me to meet that payment plan, particularly not that $300 by the 15th of this month."

You would then say, "Okay, Mr. Wilson, let's put that $300 aside for a moment. Can you make the payment of $200 by the end of this month and the $173 payment by the 10th of next month?"

If Mr. Wilson replies, "Well, I suppose I could do that," you would say, "Good. Let's see how we can work out the other $300 to get your account back to a current status. Suppose we put off the $300 payment until the end of next month. Would that be satisfactory?"

The negotiation continues with Mr. Wilson saying, "Well, I don't know. I could probably pay you $150 by the end of next month, but I couldn't pay the other $150 until my next payday after that."

You would then say, "I think that would be fine, Mr. Wilson."

Let's review what happened here. First, the financial secretary found out the part of the payment plan Mr. Wilson objected to. Then, she determined the parts he did not object to and got an agreement from him to meet those particular parts. Finally, she worked out a plan to bring his account up to date by offering him a benefit and that was, "Getting your account back into a current status." In this case the benefit of being able to receive continuing care and/or maintaining good will with the practice was subtly implied.

This case is just an example. Others may not always happen this easily. But if the steps are followed and well handled, you will be surprised at how the tough job of collection activity is made easy.

Step 8. Close the call. This is a two-part process: summarize the plan, and thank the patient. This step is very similar to Step 5 of the financial arrangement presented earlier in the book. Closing the call might go like this.

Financial secretary: "I think that would be fine, Mr. Wilson. But let's go over it again to make sure that we have it straight. You are going to send us a payment of $200 by the end of this month, and a payment of $173 by the 10th of next month. Then, by the end of the month following you will send us $150, and on your next payday, which I believe you said was on the 15th of the following month, you will send the final payment of $150 on the account. Is that correct?"

Reviewing and reaffirming the financial arrangement makes it very clear in the patient's mind that: 1) A formal agreement has just taken place, 2) You have clearly documented the terms of that agreement, and 3) It places some subtle and acceptable pressure on the patient to perform according to the terms of that agreement.

Wrapping Up After the Call

Once the phone call is completed, you still cannot "count your chickens." What you have so far is only a promise; a follow-up call may be necessary. At this point, document your conversation carefully, remembering Step 2 from your pre-call planning. Specifically document the amounts and dates you have agreed on and place that patient's follow-up card under the appropriate date in your follow-up system. Be certain to update the patient history records because as you conduct collection activity you will undoubtedly discover new information. You will discover new employers, new insurance companies, and new addresses. This recorded information ensures that you can adequately deal with this patient in the future should it become necessary. Stay on top of your accounts, then if the patient gets behind again, you will be ready for your third step in the follow-up and that is to take further action. If the patient does not make the payments as scheduled or as agreed, make another collection call, not two weeks after the patient's agreed payment date, not even a week after, but rather one day or perhaps at the most two days after the payment has become delinquent again. This is absolutely critical to the success of any collection activity and especially telephone collection activity.

This is a process of retraining your patients to learn that delinquency is unacceptable to the practice. Most health care practices have, by their lack of effective, prompt, and credible collection, trained their patients that delinquency was acceptable or, that there would be no penalty.

Again, the follow-up steps are:

1. Record your notes and document the terms of your collection activity.

2. Update your patient history records.

3. Take prompt and efficient action the moment the patient fails to keep this agreement or becomes delinquent again.

Misconceptions About Telephone Collection

Now that the proper steps for conducting telephone collection have been reviewed, let's clear up some misconceptions.

Your financial secretary may contact a patient at work, no matter what you may have heard to the contrary. She may not, however, discuss the patient's account or even the fact that your patient has an account with you with anybody other than the patient or the responsible party. It is not acceptable to contact a patient at work if that patient has specifically requested not to be contacted at work. In that event, the patient will obviously need to be contacted at home.

I am quite often asked if a patient can be called early in the morning or late in the evening. The answer is "yes," as long as the call is made during reasonable hours. The problem is the definition of "reasonable." In my opinion, a patient should not be contacted by telephone before 8:00 in the morning or after 6:00 in the evening. Although there may be a number of patients in your practice that cannot be reached during those hours, the negative aspects of contacting them early in the morning or late in the day will outweigh the advantage of being able reach the patient. If a patient cannot be reached between the hours of 8:00 in the morning and 6:00 in the evening, I suggest telephone collection is non-productive and, therefore, collection activity should be conducted by letter or in person.

Summary

This chapter assumes the financial manager or financial coordinator of the practice has thought through the collection activity options available and determined that telephone collection is the most appropriate method of collection activity for that particular patient. Telephone collection, when compared with collection activity by letter or by notes on statements or bills, will outperform the results of collection activity by letter. Collection letters are acceptable, and in some situations are absolutely necessary, but the best choice is telephone collections.

There are federal regulations dealing with collection by telephone. They are primarily those mentioned in the Fair Debt Collections Practices Act, a copy of which is available from your local credit bureau or from any local collection agency. These laws deal primarily with collection techniques utilized by banks and other lending institutions and collection agencies. However, most jurisdictions have held that any person in a collection position must follow these federal guidelines. Since these guidelines are general, and in most cases common sense, I agree and recommend you obtain a copy.

Finally, all collection phone calls will not be easy. With many calls it will be impossible to follow each of the steps. However, as long as your financial secretary understands the basics and as long as she makes an honest attempt to follow the specific steps of the collection call, you will find that her success in telephone collection will be significant. Once she becomes comfortable with telephone collection, you will find patient satisfaction will be improved, and your results in the area of increased revenue and decreased delinquency will be impressive. With lower delinquency and higher patient satisfaction will come less office stress, less workload, a higher referral rate, higher productivity per patient, higher net income, and the essence of the Zuelke & Associates purpose: a higher quality of practice life.

CHAPTER 15

COLLECTION ACTIVITY METHODS: PART II

As we begin this chapter, I want to stress again that collection activity will be effective only if your financial secretary is *willing* to use all three of the primary methods of collection — in person, by phone, and with letters.

Telephone collection activity should be the first choice for collections. She should continue to use the telephone without taking advantage of collection letters *as long as she is getting productive results.* However, merely reaching the patient by phone does not mean that she is getting productive results. "Productive" means that as a result of collection activity, the account has been brought current, or a quality financial arrangement has been made. The practice is back in a powerful relationship with your patient.

Calling a patient and getting a promise to pay only to have that promise broken is not productive results. Other examples of unproductive telephone collection are: calling the patient either at home or at work, leaving a message and not receiving a call back; calling more than twice and getting no answer; calling and reaching a patient who is rude or abusive on the telephone; calling the patient either at home or at work and having that patient say not to call him again. These are all examples of unproductive telephone collections. They are keys which indicate a switch should be made to collection activity by letter.

Effective Letter Collections

Once a decision has been made to use collection letters, there are a number of rules to follow.

Rule 1: Collection letters need to go out promptly and consistently. The moment an account has been identified as past due or the moment an agreement has been broken, collection letters should be sent.

Rule 2: Except in the initial stages of collection, ask for communication more than money. Remember the primary purpose of collections is to re-establish a quality relationship with your patients so that you are in a position to serve them and they are in a frame of mind to accept your further diagnosis. Merely sending demand letters requesting payments does not achieve this result; requesting communication rather than money usually does.

Rule 3: Indicate a sense of urgency in each letter and accelerate that urgency as subsequent letters are sent. In keeping with that goal, one collection letter must quickly follow another. Collection letters sent out at 30- to 40-day intervals will have less impact compared to well-written letters that go out at 10- to 15-day intervals.

Rule 4: Letters must be formal, typed, and sent out on formal practice stationery. Do not send out handwritten notes to patients. Do not address the letters "Dear Tom" but rather "Dear Mr. Jones." Even if this is a patient who would be called by his first name while he is in the practice, when sending a collection letter, it is time to get more formal. It is hard to create a sense of urgency when you communicate with a patient as though he were your best friend. In addition, if a patient is married and was married when the debt was incurred, then both husband and wife are equally responsible for the debt. Whether the care is provided to the children, to the husband, or to the wife individually makes no difference. Therefore, in such a situation collection letters would be addressed, "Dear Mr. and Mrs. Jones."

Rule 5: The doctor, except in rare and unusual circumstances, should not be involved in the collection process. Collection letters should be signed by the financial secretary, not by the doctor.

If your financial secretary follows these five rules when conducting letter collection activity, she will achieve a significant level of success.

In Figure 15–1 through 15–12, I have provided a series of collection letters that, in their layout, content, and method of use, follow these five rules. Note that the time from the very first letter to the very last letter is extremely condensed. The first letter goes out to a patient who is 10 days late, and the last letter goes out when the patient is just under 60 days delinquent. This may sound abrupt to you, especially if your office is typical of many health care offices: at 55 days delinquent, the first collection letter has not yet been sent. However, this method of collection activity has been tested heavily over the past 20 years in hundreds of financial institutions and hundreds more dental offices. It works quite well.

Past Due

Date________________

Occasional Oversights Do Happen

However—may we please call your attention to your past due account

PAYMENT WAS DUE		
AMOUNT DUE		

Fig. 15–1

Note that Figure 15–1 (past due notice) is a preprinted late notice. This notice is informal because it is sent to a patient who is 5 to 15 days past due. This is earlier than collection activity is normally conducted. A preprinted, informal late notice at this level of delinquency is appropriate and quite effective.

Figure 15–2 (letter #2) is the first "formal" collection letter. Note that it is on your office stationery, addressed "Dear Mr. and Mrs. Fye," and signed by the financial secretary. Note also, that this is not a hard-core, dunning letter. It is merely a formal way to let your patient know your practice is aware of his delinquency. As recommended, there is an accelerated sense of urgency, not only in the very brief time frame between the late notice and this letter (8 to 12 days) but also in the shift from a preprinted informal notice to a much more formal letter typed on office stationery.

The desired result is the patient becomes aware of an increased sense of urgency and will contact your office, make a new financial arrangement, and be restored to a positive relationship with your practice.

Assuming the patient has not responded to the previous collection letters, the account is now approximately 30 days past due (due for at least two payments). In the example I am using, two previous attempts at collection activity have been attempted (the late notice and letter #2). Now it is time to accelerate again the sense of urgency regarding this delinquency with letter #3.

ZUELKE-ASSOCIATES-INC

CONSULTANTS TO THE HEALTH CARE PROFESSION

#2

March 15, 1987

Eddie and Morta Fye
1234 Fifth Street
Anytown, OR 97000

Dear Mr. and Mrs. Fye:

Most of our patients are very busy people, and we are certain this is why you have allowed your account to become delinquent.

Since we have called this to your attention, won't you please send us a check today.

Sincerely yours,

Financial Secretary

P.O. BOX 10793 • PORTLAND, OREGON 97210 • PHONE: (503) 641-2421

Fig. 15–2. To be sent to patients who do not respond to the late notice. Send approximately 8 to 12 days after the late notice is mailed.

OR

May be sent as the initial means of collection activity. Send to a patient who is 15–30 days past due.

In reviewing letter #3 (Fig. 15–3), you should note two things. First, the top three sentences are in parentheses. This indicates the purpose of the opening statement is to review the activity that has already taken place on this account. Usually one of these first three sentences would be appropriate. However, there are some cases when none of them would be appropriate and your financial secretary would have to write a sentence. Second, note that the second paragraph starts the request for communication. It clearly advises the patient that although you would like to be paid, if he has a problem and would communicate this to you, you would be happy to work with him. Finally, the letter gives your patient the opportunity to save face and claim an oversight. But, as you well know, at 30 days delinquent and with no response to two previous attempts to collect, there is very little chance there is an oversight.

Letter #4 (Fig. 15–4) accelerates the sense of urgency we've discussed. Note the first paragraph invites him to re-establish contact with your practice and implies it still isn't too late to make an arrangement.

Note, too, that in spite of the fact that this is an aggressive letter going out to a patient who is clearly a problem (three previous contacts with no response from the patient), the letter does not ask for any money. Quite the contrary, it asks "please call us today!"

The letter in Figure 15–5 may seem in conflict with my earlier rule that the doctor never get involved in collection activity. At an appropriate time it is useful to advise the patient that you, the doctor, are aware of the delinquency. You need not request payment or suggest that the patient communicate with you about the delinquency. But neither do you allow the patient to believe that you are isolated from or unaware of this problem. Therefore, this letter is signed by you.

Note that virtually every sentence in this letter has a deeper meaning than the actual communication that is made. For instance, the first sentence advises the patient that you are not rummaging through the accounts to find out who you can write nasty letters to. However, the account is so far past due that your financial secretary has brought it to your attention. In the final paragraph you communicate to the patient that immediately ("upon receipt of this note") the patient should call the financial secretary to "make some arrangements." This statement shows that you have not taken over collection activity, but can't afford not to know about such seriously delinquent accounts.

This letter, sent out in conjunction with letter #4 , is a powerful and effective tool in your collection process.

Notice the letter in Figure 15–6 creates an extreme sense of urgency by communicating to the patient that there may be a penalty to pay for his continued delinquency. As in past letters, this letter communicates that if money is a problem, a phone call can be made and the situation can be resolved. This letter also makes the patient aware that, in addition to the

ZUELKE-ASSOCIATES-INC

CONSULTANTS TO THE HEALTH CARE PROFESSION

#3

March 25, 1987

Eddie and Morta Fye
1234 Fifth Street
Anytown, OR 97000

Dear Mr. and Mrs. Fye:

(We have sent two previous notices regarding your past-due account, yet we have not heard from you.)

(We have left three phone messages for you regarding your past-due account, yet we have not heard from you.)

(We have been reviewing your account and note that we have not received payment since [date].)

If you have encountered a problem that has made it difficult to pay this account as planned, please call our office. We will be happy to help you in any way we can.

If your lack of payment was merely an oversight, won't you please send us a check today.

Sincerely yours,

Financial Secretary

P.O. BOX 10793 • PORTLAND, OREGON 97210 • PHONE: (503) 641-2421

Fig. 15–3. Send 8 to 12 days following letter #2.

OR

Send as the initial form of collection activity to a patient who is 30+ days late.

ZUELKE-ASSOCIATES-INC

CONSULTANTS TO THE HEALTH CARE PROFESSION

#4

April 4, 1987

Eddie and Morta Fye
1234 Fifth Street
Anytown, OR 97000

Dear Mr. and Mrs. Fye:

In spite of repeated requests from this office, we have neither received payment nor have we received a call to explain a difficulty you may have in making a payment on your account.

We are rapidly coming to the conclusion that you do not wish to cooperate with this office in resolving what must be a problem.

If this is not the case, please call us today! You will find that we are still willing to help in any realistic manner.

Sincerely yours,

Financial Secretary

P.O. BOX 10793 • PORTLAND, OREGON 97210 • PHONE: (503) 641-2421

Fig. 15–4. Send 8 to 12 days after the #3 letter

OR

extremely rare and unusual circumstances, send as the first form of collection activity to a patient who is severely delinquent.

ZUELKE-ASSOCIATES-INC

CONSULTANTS TO THE HEALTH CARE PROFESSION

#5

April 4, 1987

Eddie and Morta Fye
1234 Fifth Street
Anytown, OR 97000

Dear Mr. and Mrs. Fye:

My financial secretary has advised me that your account has become seriously delinquent. I am sure that when you were in for your dental care you did not intend that your account be handled in this manner.

Unfortunately, and especially in these times, I am unable to continue to carry any accounts in a delinquent status.

Upon receipt of this note will you please call ______________ to make some arrangements. You will find that she is willing to cooperate with any realistic payment arrangement.

Sincerely yours,

Doctor

P.O. BOX 10793 • PORTLAND, OREGON 97210 • PHONE: (503) 641-2421

Fig. 15–5. Send out in conjunction with the previous letter in Fig. 15–4. Mail the same day in separate envelopes.

penalty (no longer being able to continue to carry the account), there would be an advantage to paying (maintaining a good credit rating).

After receiving a letter like Figure 15–6, especially in light of having received several similar letters over a very short period of time, a patient should be very clear that the time for continued collection activity is rapidly coming to a close, leaving only one final result.

In the event the patient who is past due is in active orthodontic treatment, then this is an appropriate time for your financial secretary to explain to your patient that receipt of continued, progressive orthodontic care is not an option if he is going to continue to be delinquent and/or if he continues to respond inappropriately (or does not respond at all) to the collection activity. Except in rare and unusual circumstances, an orthodontist or a dentist doing orthodontics has no obligation to continue to provide orthodontic care to a patient who will not handle his account appropriately. Placing a patient in maintenance for 30 days (maximum of 60 days) is a powerful and effective collection tool that will, in most cases, resolve the delinquency problem.

Remember the lesson learned earlier — commitment to be *as uncomfortable as it takes* in order to get the desired result. Postponing active treatment, removing braces, and dismissing a patient from your practice are all uncomfortable steps. However, experience in this area has shown that your willingness to dismiss a patient from the practice for his inappropriate behavior (financially or clinically) makes it unlikely you will actually have to dismiss a patient from the practice.

Let me caution you that one of the laws governing collection activity is that you must not threaten a patient with an activity you do not fully intend to carry out. Do not threaten to take a patient out of treatment, or threaten to dismiss a patient from the practice, unless you intend to do so. If your commitment is to create quality within your practice, then you must be willing to send and follow through on the #6 (ortho) letter (Fig. 15–7).

Two recommendations:

1. Maintenance will almost always be limited to 30 days and in no case should maintenance be extended beyond 60 days.

2. The doctor and clinical staff must support the financial secretary by only checking for broken wires, loose bands, etc. Again, no progressive treatment.

You will recall that the purpose of collection activity is to resolve the problem: there is a patient who is in a negative relationship with the practice. You hope the resolution comes by having the account paid in full. If not that, you hope the resolution will come from negotiating a new, mutually agreeable financial agreement with the patient. But the third choice, which is a perfectly acceptable if not desirable choice, is dismissal of the patient from the practice and writing the account off the books.

ZUELKE-ASSOCIATES-INC

CONSULTANTS TO THE HEALTH CARE PROFESSION

#6

April 9, 1987

Eddie and Morta Fye
1234 Fifth Street
Anytown, OR 97000

Dear Mr. and Mrs. Fye:

Your lack of communication with our office regarding your past-due account concerns us. Very shortly we will be in a position where we are no longer able to continue to carry your account. Please consider your future credit standing with this office and with the community.

We will expect to hear from you no later than ____(5 days)____.

Sincerely yours,

Financial Secretary

P.O. BOX 10793 • PORTLAND, OREGON 97210 • PHONE: (503) 641-2421

Fig. 15–6. Send 5 to 8 days following letters #4 and 5.

ZUELKE-ASSOCIATES-INC

CONSULTANTS TO THE HEALTH CARE PROFESSION

#6 Ortho
Send Certified - Keep a Copy

April 9, 1987

Eddie and Morta Fye
1234 Fifth Street
Anytown, OR 97000

Dear Mr. and Mrs. Fye:

Your lack of communication with our office regarding your past-due account concerns us. If we do not receive the payment due shortly, we will have no choice but to discontinue further treatment of (name) .

We have no desire to deny needed orthodontic treatment, and to allow you time to bring this account current or to make an appropriate financial arrangement with this office, we will continue to see (name) as a maintenance patient only for the next _____ days. During this period, there will be no tooth movement, and the time for completion of treatment will be extended. If by (date) , the account has not been brought current or an appropriate financial arrangement has not been made, further treatment of (name) will be discontinued.

Please call our office immediately if you have any questions.

Sincerely yours,

Doctor

P.O. BOX 10793 • PORTLAND, OREGON 97210 • PHONE: (503) 641-2421

Fig. 15–7. Send to a patient in orthodontic treatment who does not respond to the 4th and 5th letters, approximately 10 to 15 days following #4 and #5.

My experience shows that if collection activity is conducted as explained in this and previous chapters, and if it has been done consistently and with credibility, you will rarely have cases which reach the point where the letter in Figure 15–8 would be necessary. However, if your commitment in the practice is to create true quality of life and you accept that to mean there would be little or no delinquency, you must be willing to dismiss a patient from the practice, especially when that patient has shown an unwillingness to work within the parameters your practice has established.

It is acceptable, legal, moral, and ethical to dismiss a patient from your practice. Your obligation is to give that patient notice. As you can see, this letter gives notice.

An important distinction to make: This letter does not advise the patient that future care will be provided on a cash-only basis. This letter formally dismisses the patient from the practice and advises him that future care, other than emergency care over the next 30 days, will not be provided at all.

Once this letter has been sent, the account balance will be written off the books and no further collection activity will be conducted.

After receiving #7 ortho letter (Fig. 15–9), it should be clear to your patients that you have their best interest as your primary concern and that at this point you only want communication.

As stated in the explanation for the #6 ortho letter and as mentioned earlier in this book, occasionally it will be necessary to dismiss an uncooperative patient from your practice. Except in rare, technical cases, you cannot be expected to provide continuing care to an uncooperative patient. You have an obligation to your own personal well-being, and you have an obligation to the well-being of your other patients to maintain a healthy, profitable practice. You cannot afford to continue to contribute to patients who refuse to contribute to you in kind.

Two recommendations regarding letter #8 ortho (Fig. 15–10):

1. Be sure it is sent certified, return receipt requested.

2. After receiving this letter, if your patient calls and wants to make amends, the financial secretary must not make any financial arrangement that is not absolutely and completely realistic — a financial arrangement that will bring the entire delinquent amount current in a reasonable period of time (one to two months).

Occasionally your office will receive a payment from a patient that is either a token payment ($10 or $20) or is a payment that will not amortize (pay off) the account balance in a reasonable time period. For instance, a $50 payment may not be token, but if the account balance is $2,000, $50 is certainly an unrealistic monthly payment.

In such a situation the first choice would be to conduct collection activity by telephone and handle the delinquency in that manner. However, if telephone collection has been determined to be ineffective or unproductive, then a collection letter such as the one in Figure 15–11 must be sent. Notice two things:

ZUELKE-ASSOCIATES-INC

CONSULTANTS TO THE HEALTH CARE PROFESSION

Dismissal letter

April 30, 1987

Eddie and Morta Fye
1234 Fifth Street
Anytown, OR 97000

Dear Mr. and Mrs. Fye:

Due to (your inability to handle your financial obligation to this office in a satisfactory manner) (or your numerous cancellations/no-shows) (or your general lack of cooperation with our office policies and procedures), we will no longer be able to provide dental services to you or to members of your immediate family.

Since continuing dental care is extremely important for your general health and well-being, we recommend that you seek the services of another dentist immediately. We will continue to provide dental care on an emergency-only basis for thirty days from the date of this letter. After (date), further treatment will not be provided.

The balance of your account is $_______. (If, in the future, you should make the decision to take care of this balance by payment in full, we will again be able to provide dental care although it would be on a cash-only basis.) (or, if you do not want to see this patient again - We request that you contact our office immediately to discuss a financial arrangement on your account balance of $_______.)

If you are unable to locate another dentist to serve your needs, please contact this office. We will be pleased to recommend another dentist to you.

Sincerely yours,

John Q. Jones, DDS

P.O. BOX 10793 ▪ PORTLAND, OREGON 97210 ▪ PHONE: (503) 641-2421

Fig. 15–8. Send to a patient 10 to 15 days following letter #6.

ZUELKE-ASSOCIATES-INC

CONSULTANTS TO THE HEALTH CARE PROFESSION

#7 Ortho

April 23, 1987

Eddie and Morta Fye
1234 Fifth Street
Anytown, OR 97000

Dear Mr. and Mrs. Fye:

It has been two weeks since our letter advising you that _(name's)_ treatment has temporarily been placed on hold pending a satisfactory resolution of the delinquency problem with your account.

Our purpose in this practice is to provide health care to our patients, and we are unhappy as well as uncomfortable at the thought of having to discontinue progressive orthodontic care.

Please respond immediately, therefore, to our letter of ________________ so that we may proceed with treatment and bring your orthodontic treatment to an excellent final result.

Sincerely yours,

Financial Secretary

P.O. BOX 10793 • PORTLAND, OREGON 97210 • PHONE: (503) 641-2421

Fig 15–9. Send out approximately two weeks following the #6 ortho letter.

ZUELKE-ASSOCIATES-INC

CONSULTANTS TO THE HEALTH CARE PROFESSION

#8 Ortho
Discontinuation of Treatment
Send Certified - Keep a Copy

June 23, 1987

Eddie and Morta Fye
1234 Fifth Street
Anytown, OR 97000

Dear Mr. and Mrs. Fye:

As we advised in our letter of __(date)__ and in view of your continuing lack of cooperation with regard to your financial obligation to this office, I am hereby advising you that I shall terminate treatment of __(name)__ thirty days from the date of this letter.

In my opinion, __(name)__ can benefit from continued orthodontic care, and I urge you to seek the services of another orthodontist.

If you decide not to have another orthodontist take over treatment within the next thirty days, I recommend that you contact my office to have the appliances removed since there may be health problems from wearing appliances without periodic maintenance and adjustment. These potential problems include: decalcification of teeth, increased risk of cavities, and the possibility of injury to soft tissues of the mouth from loose or broken appliances.

Your account balance has been adjusted to reflect this early discontinuation of treatment. Your new balance, for which you are still responsible, is $________.

Sincerely,

Doctor

P.O. BOX 10793 • PORTLAND, OREGON 97210 • PHONE: (503) 641-2421

Fig. 15–10. Send out 30 days following the #6 letter (60 days in rare cases).

1. The statement "We are unable to continue to accept" and
2. "If you have encountered a problem . . . please call our office."

As with regular collection letters, the message must convey that your office is always open to a patient's problems and working out a mutually agreeable financial arrangement.

Many of you right now are in some state of shock. But that is correct; the payment in this situation would be returned to the patient. Remember, the purpose for conducting collection activity is not to collect a payment but to resolve the problem. Another purpose is to educate patients that they must operate within the parameters your practice has established and that operating otherwise is not acceptable.

Partial payment letter #1 (Fig. 15–11) advised the patient that although one partial payment was accepted, no further payments of this nature could be accepted. That's why partial payment letter #2 (Fig. 15–12) rejects this payment. If another token or partial payment were accepted and another collection letter written, the office would have no credibility with the patient. He would, in fact, have been taught that he can get away with doing exactly what he feels like doing. The delinquency problem would not be resolved. It would be worse. By returning a patient's payment, the staff demonstrates in no uncertain terms that they mean what they say. This brings the issue to a close.

If you truly believe that "something is better than nothing," then you are reading the wrong book. Sending money back to a patient is difficult, but may be the activity that resolves the problem and brings the patient back into relationship with the practice. If not, it will at the very least, accelerate a process of ultimate dismissal which might have happened anyway.

Once this letter has been sent out, the patient is delinquent with no recent payment. The next form of collection activity that would be appropriate (assuming, as always, that the telephone has been deemed unacceptable) would be the #4 and #5 letters.

Providing Treatment For Charity Cases

It's time to take a moment to explain the alternative to collection activity as aggressive as I have just described. We know that in the majority of cases, delinquency is not justified. The patients could pay in a realistic manner if they chose to. The problem is a matter of priorities.

Once in a while, however, you will be able to document a bona fide charity case — a situation where the patient or responsible party is truly in a position where he is incapable of making realistic or appropriate payments on an account.

There are two factors to consider when confronted with a case such as this. On one hand, it is not realistic for a doctor to provide free health care to every person who gets into a financial situation that prevents him from paying for health care. On the other hand, all health care providers have an obligation to provide a certain amount of free or "charity" health care.

ZUELKE-ASSOCIATES-INC

CONSULTANTS TO THE HEALTH CARE PROFESSION

Partial Payment #1

March 15, 1987

Eddie and Morta Fye
1234 Fifth Street
Anytown, OR 97000

Dear Mr. and Mrs. Fye:

Thank you for your check in the amount of $______ which we have applied to your account.

In accordance with our office credit policies and without prior approval, we are unable to continue to accept payments in this amount. Please be certain that all future payments are in the amount of $______.

If you have encountered a problem that will prevent you from making payments on this account as requested, please call our office. We will be happy to help you in any way we can.

Sincerely yours,

Financial Secretary

P.O. BOX 10793 • PORTLAND, OREGON 97210 • PHONE: (503) 641-2421

Fig. 15–11. Send to any patient who makes a payment less than agreed to or less than is appropriate given the size of the balance.

ZUELKE·ASSOCIATES·INC

CONSULTANTS TO THE HEALTH CARE PROFESSION

Partial Payment #2

April 1, 1987

Eddie and Morta Fye
1234 Fifth Street
Anytown, OR 97000

Dear Mr. and Mrs. Fye:

Thank you for your payment of $______ which we received this morning. Unfortunately, without prior approval and as we advised in our letter of __(date)__, we are unable to accept payments in this amount.

Accordingly, we are returning your check and request that you send a minimum payment of $______ immediately. If you have encountered a problem that will prevent you from paying this account as requested, please call us today. We will be pleased to help you in any way we can.

Sincerely yours,

Financial Secretary

P.O. BOX 10793 ▪ PORTLAND, OREGON 97210 ▪ PHONE: (503) 641-2421

Fig. 15–12. Send to a patient if, after the first partial payment letter was sent, you receive another less-than-adequate payment.

The amount of free health care provided can be decided only by the doctor. Once a financial secretary has determined that a patient is incapable of paying for health care that has been or is about to be provided, the decision on doing free work should be made by the doctor. However, I strongly encourage doctors to listen to and follow the recommendations of their financial secretaries, who are in a more powerful position to make an unemotional decision regarding this patient.

One other rule to follow — as painful as it may be — is that the account balance *must* be written off the books if care is going to be provided to a patient who cannot pay for the treatment. There is no situation that I can think of where token or partial payments are appropriate.

Summary

Following the guidelines and using the collection letters presented in this chapter, you will see an incredible shift from the way collection activity has typically been conducted in your practice. Leaving accounts on the books for months and even years without problem resolution has caused negative energy among the staff, the doctor, and the patients. Now your practice has, over a short period of time, either collected the account and brought the patient back into relationship with the practice or dismissed the patient from the practice. Either way, the practice has enjoyed a powerful resolution through the collection process.

CHAPTER 16

ACCOUNTING SYSTEMS

A common situation I see as a consultant is an office utilizing a computerized system they hate and they want something else. Or an office utilizing a manual system they hate, and they think they need a computer. I also see offices operating at $20,000 a month but think they could get to $30,000 if they only had a computer. I have other clients producing over $100,000 a month who utilize a manual pegboard posting system. There is no evidence in the dental community to support the belief that being computerized or not being computerized has any significant impact on the growth, profitability, or the efficiency of the practice.

My recommendation to my clients is extremely simple: that they have an efficient and well-organized accounting system. This can be an in-house computer, a pegboard posting system augmented by a batch processing service, or a straight manual pegboard system. All three systems can and do work, and all three systems can and do fail. It depends on the level of commitment to implement whatever system is being used.

I recognize these last statements do not sound like much of a recommendation or guideline, and this book is supposed to be about guidelines. The best that I can do is give you the benefit of my experience seeing many dental offices operate.

My observation is that being computerized, either with an in-house system or with a batch processing system, allows you to be more efficient in the implementation of the recommendations I have made in this book. If you are computerized or if you are on a computer-generated pegboard system (batch processing service), you can charge interest on open accounts and send monthly statements more efficiently and easily than you can on a system that is manual in nature. Also, embezzlement controls are simpler to implement when you have a computer-based system.

Whether you choose to utilize an in-house system or a batch billing service is purely a matter of personal choice. I have seen very little difference in value between the two.

CHAPTER 17

IMPLEMENTING BONUS SYSTEMS

It is every businessman's dream — and this certainly includes doctors — to have a staff that is talented, motivated, and committed, a staff with impeccable integrity. Many have succeeded in surrounding themselves with such a staff. These offices achieve outstanding results: excellent productivity, excellent collections, and excellent service due to the efforts of a fine staff. Members of such a staff go out of their way to contribute to the well-being of the practice. They do so not for a specific reward but because of their own level of integrity. Doing well or going "all out" for an employer is very satisfying to this type of staff member.

Even with this kind of staff, it is clear that appropriate acknowledgment produces even greater effort and even greater results. I am referring to an incentive plan, commonly called a bonus system.

How to Implement a Bonus System

There are numerous bonus systems in use in this country. Some work better than others. I am not going to present a "recommended" bonus system to you, but I will suggest a few criteria for establishing your bonus system. These suggestions ensure the success of a bonus system. A bonus system must:

1. Reward the staff for *superior* performance.
2. *Motivate* the staff to work for that superior performance.
3. Be a "*win*" for the doctor and a "*win*" for the staff. (It takes little imagination to design a bonus system that is great for the staff and lousy for the doctor. Conversely, many bonus systems are great for the doctor and lousy for the staff. An incentive plan must be a win for both parties. Otherwise, it will end up being a loser for both.)

Some Dos and Don'ts

There are some "dos" and "don'ts" to remember when implementing a bonus system.

* DO base your system on performance your staff has direct control over.
* DO NOT base your bonus system on net income.

Many doctors like to base a bonus on net income. The problem with this should be apparent. Except in minor circumstances, the staff has almost no control over net income. Some doctors run many personal purchases through the practice. This affects net income. In addition, it is unfair for the staff to lose a bonus because the doctor decided to carpet the floor, buy a new dental chair, or hire a consultant. However, the staff, to a greater degree, does have control over gross production and gross collections. Therefore, a bonus system should be based on that.

* DO pay bonuses earned promptly.
* DO NOT include bonuses in regular paychecks.

There is an old adage: "Fast pay makes fast friends." This certainly applies with staff bonuses and incentive plans. Often administrative and clinical staff spend the majority (if not all) of their net income on household expenses. Therefore, a bonus included in a paycheck will end up being spent on monthly expenses, and the value of that bonus will be less apparent to your staff.

The most valued way of paying a bonus is to 1) pay it within one to five days of the end of the month in which the bonus was earned, and 2) to have the bonus checks paid to the staff totally independent of their paychecks. Many doctors actually write a total check, go to the bank and cash it, and pay their employees in cash. This is highly motivating and certainly is appreciated by many staff members. (Caution: Be certain that this money is included in your employees' W-2s as wages earned during the year.)

* DO pay bonuses based on one month's performance.
* DO NOT pay bonuses based on quarterly, semi-annual, or annual results.

Remember, the purpose of a bonus system is not just to reward the staff for superior performance but also to provide a level of motivation. Bonus systems should encourage your staff to strive for superior performance.

I have observed many clients that pay a bonus based on quarterly results and some on semi-annual results. The problem here is apparent. If January is a horrible month simply because it was a horrible month, or because the doctor went on vacation, or because computer conversion caused turmoil in the office thereby reducing production, or if for any reason production is inhibited, the staff will be less motivated going into February. They know they must overcome the huge deficit created in January—a deficit perhaps they had no control over.

* DO work out terms of the incentive plan with your staff.
* DO NOT make unilateral decisions regarding your bonus system.

The key here is to have an incentive plan that is a win for your staff as well as a win for you. To establish this win/win plan, you must work out the terms of your agreement with the staff. They must be able to bring up their concerns, their objections, or their suggestions and have them considered in the development of an effective incentive plan. Remember a bonus system which sounds good for the doctor may not sound good for the staff and vice versa.

* DO establish a date when the existing bonus system will be reviewed and possibly revised.
* DO NOT establish your bonus system "until further notice."

Many bonus systems are effective only during periods of rapid growth and others are effective only for an office that has reached a plateau. Therefore, any bonus system should have a beginning date and an ending date at which time the bonus system will be reviewed. The existing system may be renewed in its current form assuming that there is agreement between the doctor and the staff, or it may be completely revised depending on the particular office circumstances at the time.

* DO pay bonuses to the entire team.
* DO NOT exclude certain staff members.

I have always felt it was unfortunate that some practices choose to exclude certain staff members from the bonus. The reasons commonly given are: "They are only part-time," "They are just lab persons," "She is a high school girl who works only a few hours a month." Every person on your staff, whether full-time or part-time, does the job for which they are hired. The fact a part-time high school girl may not be contributing at the same level as a dental hygienist should be insignificant. That part-time high school girl is theoretically contributing to the maximum she was asked to contribute. Therefore, she deserves the exact same share of the bonus (relative to the hours worked) as would a hygienist or an office manager. The bonus should not be based on the value of the job or the person to the practice. Rather, base the bonus system solely on the number of hours worked. If an individual employee needs more acknowledgment because they are of more value to the practice or they are more committed or they are working harder, that type of acknowledgment should be handled through salary increases.

Summary

Whether you agree with what you have just read or not, one question that is probably on your mind is, why in the world is there a chapter on bonus systems in a book on credit management and accounts receivable control? The answer is very simple. By now you are certainly aware of the complexity of credit management in a health care practice. Maintaining a practice with a very high quality of life as well as a high profit margin cannot be done by a doctor on his own. It takes a doctor working with a strong, motivated team willing to work as hard as it takes to obtain these results. A properly designed incentive plan can provide significant assistance in developing and maintaining your team.

Conclusion

Well, you have seen and read about the whole system. You have learned about and should understand the general importance of credit management for the dental office. You have learned the importance of identifying your quality patients, of nurturing and supporting them in every way possible. And you have learned the value of controlling the patients who will not or cannot contribute to your well-being.

I imagine that if you are reading this section, you are probably a financial secretary, the doctor long since having given up reading once the book got to the technical details — the "nuts and bolts." It is just as well because it is the financial secretary who is going to make this system work.

I want to remind you that just as you would eat an elephant one bite at a time, so also should the credit management policies you have read about be implemented one step at a time. With true commitment on your part and with appropriate support from the rest of the staff and from the doctor, you will soon be well on your way to reaching your vision.

INDEX

Q

R